A Treasure Chest of Teaching Wisdom

I Teach First Grade!

Ellen A. Thompson

Crystal Springs
BOOKS

Published by
Crystal Springs Books • Peterborough, New Hampshire
1-800-321-0401 • www.crystalsprings.com

© 2001 Crystal Springs Books

Printed in the United States of America

Published by Crystal Springs Books
75 Jaffrey Road
PO Box 500
Peterborough, NH 03458
1-800-321-0401
www.sde.com, www.crystalsprings.com

U.S. Cataloging-in-Publication Data
(Library of Congress Standards)

Thompson, Ellen A., 1955-
    I teach first grade! : a treasure chest of teaching wisdom / Ellen
A. Thompson. —1st. ed.
[240] p. : ill. ; cm. (I teach series)
Includes bibliographical references and index.
Summary : All aspects of teaching first grade, including creating the
learning environment, time saving tips and techniques, developing curriculum,
performing assessment and the school-home connection.
ISBN 1-884548-35-0
1. Education, Primary. 2. Teaching. 3. First grade (Education). I.
Title. 2. Series.
372.241 21 2001 CIP
2001131710

Vice President, Merchandise and Publishing: Lorraine Walker
Editor and Publishing Projects Coordinator: Meredith Reed O'Donnell
Illustrations: Patrick Belfiori
Cover, book design, and production: Soosen Dunholter

This book is dedicated to:

my son, Christopher, whose constant refrain, "So, when are
you going to write a book?" finally got my goat!

my husband, Jim, whose excitement about this book is
definitely equal to my own and whose commitment to the
process came in the forms of editor, writer,
graphic artist, and even confidant and counselor

my friend and colleague Annie, who helped make all my
teaching dreams a reality for the children in Room 6

my friend Susan Ohanian—who was the first to say,
"Write a book."

and my students—this book's for you!

Table of Contents

Introduction, by Ellen A. Thompson

CHAPTER 1: Create the Perfect Classroom Environment

CHAPTER 2: Classroom Management Tips and Techniques

CHAPTER 3: Time Management Tips

CHAPTER 4: Widely Held Expectations for First Graders: Benchmarks, State Standards, and Assessment Tools

CHAPTER 5: Explore Your Curriculum

 Book icon indicates recommended resources.

INTRODUCTION

I can still remember the first day of school in my own classroom, Room 6. I had worked part time for two years, just waiting for an opening at the school in which I had student taught. My principal believed in waiting for just the right position to open up for just the right person, and he believed the classroom he had assigned me was the perfect match. I can still remember my panic as those sixteen students walked through MY door.

I had spent all summer working on Room 6. It had captivating bulletin boards, hands-on games, and neat piles of basal readers complete with their workbooks. And then, in they walked. I knew at first glance those neat piles were not going to help me in all the ways I would need during that first year. I had inherited the "transitional" second grade from a woman considered an institution in the school district. Her shoes would be hard to fill. But I saw it as a great compliment that my principal had saved this position just for me. As I looked over these children, however, I began to wonder if it was because no one else would take the class! These were the students who had "almost" passed first grade, but not quite. They had potential, but the potential had not yet emerged. In reality, these were all the remedial students from both ends of town.

I began to naively think, "This will work." These students are all working at the same level, right? We could do everything "whole" class. My bulletin boards would work. My games would come in handy for extra practice. Those neat piles of basals would fit perfectly—high interest selections that they were. I quickly discovered, however, that every child in the classroom was different. Some smelled of barnyard; others I could hardly understand because of their obscure grammar patterns; others were older, larger; still others were nervous about having been brought to a new school. The only thing they had in common was that they were all unique!

I could feel my plan crumbling. I found myself trying the methods of that teacher who had preceded me and I found that it didn't work. My one reading group turned into two groups, then three . . . four . . . sixteen, almost before my very eyes. I ignored the manual and began teaching my way, and I quickly became aware that "my way" looked and sounded very different from the classrooms surrounding my room. For instance, I found I could learn many things right alongside my students—phonics rules made more sense when talked about and discussed as they were being used. I began to close my door so the other teachers wouldn't see me learning from and with my students. I closed my door and began to discover the process of change that would mold me into the teacher I am today.

This book is about that change. My classroom door is no longer closed. I know now that my way was right even twenty years ago—I just didn't have or know of a model to help me affirm what I was discovering with my students. This book is meant to be such a model for educators eager to grow and change with their students.

*   *   *

I remember that first year vividly. It was a real awakening for me. I remember being overwhelmed with the importance of "doing it right." And what was "right"? There didn't seem to be a simple answer. I talked with colleagues, I read, I took courses, and still I could not "get it right." I still had questions. I still felt like I could be doing more.

Twenty years later, I know that I don't have all the answers. Some days I "do it" very well, and others I do not. I still read, talk with colleagues, take courses, and reflect on the doings of my children and myself. Over the years I have learned there is no easy way to teach. There is no one "right way." But the best teachers are constantly learning from one another through lessons learned from their classroom-based research. For this reason I offer *I Teach First Grade! A Treasure Chest of Teaching Wisdom*. It is a means to help foster that learning process for new and experienced teachers alike. I know I learn best from what has worked in real classrooms recounted by real teachers. I am a real teacher. This is my learning: from my classroom to yours.

Sincerely,

Ellen

CREATE THE PERFECT CLASSROOM ENVIRONMENT

Classrooms should be colorful, creative, print-rich environments, built and designed to allow movement. They should contain quiet areas, table space, and large meeting places where the entire class can gather each day. In many public schools, unfortunately, classroom space is confined to a square, with little thought given to its interesting nooks and crannies. Have fun and be creative with how you use the spaces within the basic "box" shape.

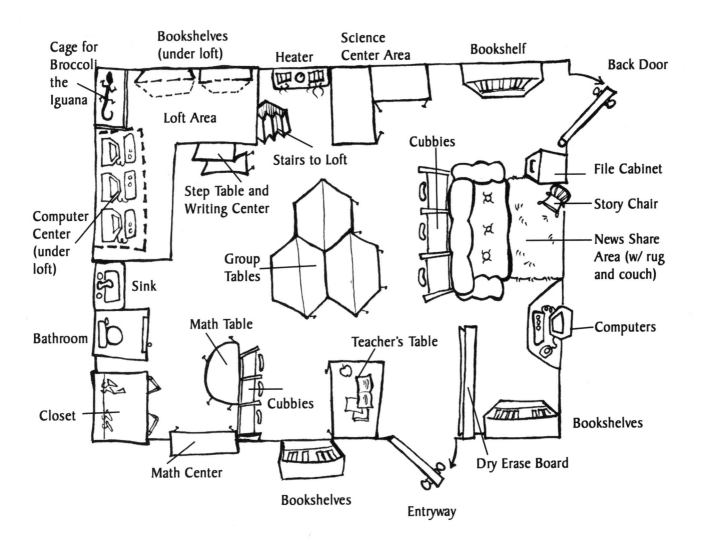

As you design your room, remember that everyone will benefit from a smooth traffic pattern. Think about all the places your students will travel within the classroom during any given day and consider carefully where items will be placed. Putting the electric pencil sharpener near your small-group work area, for example, may not be a good idea.

As you collect furniture for your classroom, think on the wild side. I have seen classrooms with
- lofts
- bunk beds
- beanbag chairs
- claw-foot bathtubs filled with pillows

Such fun, comfortable places encourage children to pick out a book, relax, and read.

Ceiling and Walls

Each year my room begins empty of ceiling and wall art, but once the students and I start creating, the classroom ceiling and walls take on a whole new shape. Use your students' artwork to transform your room from one that you are simply sharing with students to one that is truly theirs. Be careful not to clutter these areas, however. It's fun to decorate, but don't bombard children with too much color, print, and artwork. Arrange things so that everyone can appreciate and utilize these creations (e.g., word wall, theme-related work).

Room 6 without students and artwork!

*Room 6 **with** students and artwork!*

Bulletin Boards: Working Murals

Most classrooms are equipped with one or more bulletin boards. These can be used as
- display areas
- learning centers
- instructional backdrops

Below are three fun board ideas that you and your students can create together.

A Welcome Board displays students' names and gives a little peek into our yearlong theme.
Can you guess what we'll be studying?

Welcome Board

At the beginning of each school year, I usually design a "Welcome Board" that displays each student's name and one or more theme-related pictures. This display immediately lets the student know that s/he is in the right place, and it gives a sneak preview as to what we might be studying during the year. It's exciting to watch this display grow throughout the fall as we add ourselves to the picture. Together we are creating a working mural.

Instructional Board

In addition to the Welcome Board, I reserve one classroom bulletin board for instructional purposes. This board covers one side of our rug-area meeting place, an area where the entire class gathers to read aloud, share news, and take part in other group-related activities. Since I do not make use of a blackboard, I use large paper to record our many conversations (I write in large print), thus creating a hard copy for us to refer back to throughout the year. These copies are then hung around the room or even bound together into impromptu class "big books," which become part of our Room 6 library. The children love to read over what we have been discussing in the classroom, and often they will even "play school" while here at school!

News Share area of Room 6.

Informational Boards

My other boards serve as information areas. For example, I may hang posters that advocate proper nutrition or display theme-related pictures that show Mayan weaving patterns. These boards are meant to jog students' interests and prompt them to ask questions. And of course we create many more display boards throughout the school year, some with posters that have been purchased, but many with student artwork. I strive for each child to be represented, and most importantly, I do not showcase only the "best" work in the classroom. First graders are extremely sensitive, as are we adults, and they are often performing their best; it's just that one child's best might look a little different from another child's best. What's important is that each student does his/her *personal* best!

Question & Answer

How do I bind the news sheets together?

Bind pages together by following the steps below:

1. Put your book pages in order
2. Take the last page first—face up—and lay it on a table top
3. Take a 2" wide roll of clear tape and tape the left-hand side of the page to the table, half on the page/half off the page
4. Lay the next page on top of this page
5. Tape this page to the table
6. Continue taping all the pages, including the front cover
7. Trim tape off the top and bottom of pages
8. Pull the bundle of pages off the table
9. Cover the sticky-tape edge with another piece of clear tape, or fold tape over to back
10. Read the book!

If you wish to bind pages back-to-back, simply:

1. Place paper on table (start with page one)
2. Take masking or clear tape and tape all four edges of one page
3. Lift from the table
4. Flip over onto table
5. Place the back side of the page to follow on top of the back side of the previous page
6. Fold tape over
7. Trim accordingly

The pages are now bound, and the layers of tape on the left-hand side have formed a spine for your book (which will last a long time!).

Note: You may bind any type of student-created or class-made book together by following the previous directions. You can also bind pages together (single-side or back-to-back) by using metal rings, which you can purchase at your local paper supply store or through a supply catalog. And don't forget, if your school has a laminating machine, you can help preserve smaller books by giving them this protective seal. Your students will love how professional their books look and feel!

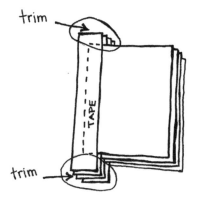

Floor Space

Tables and Desks

Think about how you want your classroom to look and consider what types of furniture might be available to use. Start with tables and desks. Tables are fun because they give the classroom a "community" feel and allow students to share materials and work with table partners. Desks, on the other hand, tend to separate students, but can be moved into doubles, squares, or rectangles to minimize distance. Often the best solution is a combination of the two tables for group work, and desks, strategically placed around the room, for quiet, work-by-yourself areas.

Shelves

Tubs and crate structures at student eye level create visible and easily accessible shelves for your book collection. Arrange books in plastic washtubs or crates. This setup allows children to flip through the titles, seeing, as they go, the front covers. Avoid shelves where only the spines of the books are visible, because six-year-olds are just like adults—they choose the books they want to read by the author, cover art, and theme.

Room 6 students busy at work.

Question & Answer

Do you assign seats to your students?

This decision is up to the individual teacher. I do not assign seats to my students, but I talk with them about finding a "good place for you [the students]" when they are first searching for a place to sit. Students usually know when they can handle sitting next to a best friend and when they might need a quieter place. You might also allow students to choose their own seats, then create a seating chart from their choices. Now you have allowed for their input, but you also know where to find them during the day!

Flower Box Shelves

I took the shelving design one step further. Knowing I had an exorbitant book collection that would easily overtake my entire boxlike classroom, I designed holders that could be placed flat on the tops of cubbies or on any other surface in the classroom. (For directions on how to make these boxes, see page 209.) I borrowed the design from a basic "flower box." Later, I added a bottom to these boxes, which gave them weight and made moving around the classroom collection much easier. By yourself or with your students, help brighten up your classroom each year by painting these boxes different colors!

Book storage units display book covers first, making it easy for students to flip through titles and select the book of their choice.

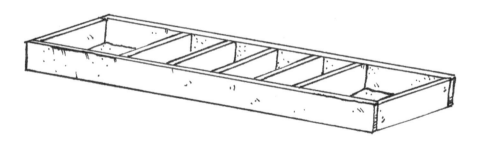

Cubbies

Often-used classroom materials should be in easy reach for your first graders. Cubbies are just perfect for this type of storage! Cubbies may be purchased through school supply catalogs, but most catalog cubbies are expensive and inefficient. The best cubbies I have seen are those designed by classroom teachers. The school custodian built my cubbies, and in some school districts teachers work with local vocational-education or high school technology-program students, who are often happy to lend a hand.

When designing cubbies, remember that they should be at student eye level and should contain a large storage area, as your first graders come with lunch boxes, extra sweaters, and lots of cool stuff to share. And here's a hint: cubbies on wheels are a good alternative to stationary holders; they can even be used to divide your room into different spaces.

Cubbies are also a good way to teach organizational skills and responsibility. Talk with students about why it is important to return belongings to cubbies and how to store them neatly. Care of personal and room materials will help students become more invested in their classroom environment.

Question & Answer

What are some alternatives to cubbies?

Since classroom space is always at a premium, teachers have devised lots of interesting ways to solve storage problems.

Here are some ideas:

- Plastic tubs

- Built-in shelves that hold tubs or crates

- Behind-the-Chair Bags: These bags resemble backpacks and hang behind students' seats. The bags have an opening at the top and two straps sewn onto the back. Ask a parent or classroom volunteer if they might be willing to help construct these bags.

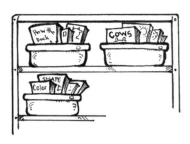

Common Meeting Place

A meeting place is a must for the first-grade classroom. If possible, your meeting area should be big enough for the children to form a circle, as class gatherings are best when everyone can see one another.

Create your meeting place using these common elements:
- book easel stand or bulletin board where you want the children to focus for short instructional lessons and/or directions
- a rug to make the space more comfortable and to define the area in which you want students to gather

Classroom Meeting Area

The rug and couch make this a comfortable place for students to work together or read quietly alone.

Question & Answer

What meeting-area expectations do you create with students?

When my students come to the rug area for an instructional lesson or to read aloud, they know to follow certain behaviors.

Design a list of appropriate meeting-area behaviors with your students. Below is a list I created with my Room 6 students.
- Sit quietly on the rug
- Sit flat
- Eyes and ears on whomever is talking
- Face forward
- Keep hands in your lap or at your side

Creating a Loft

When I added a loft to my classroom, I gained valuable space. Actually, it is hard to imagine all those years I taught without this structure. My husband built our loft with materials purchased through a PTO mini-grant. With approximately $300.00 in hand and a helpful hubby, the loft became a reality. Below are some of the ways we used our loft in Room 6:

- Quiet reading space
- Small-group meetings
- Puppet shows
- Book storage
- Classroom computer workspace: Computers can be used under the loft, giving this space a private, office-area feel.

Discuss "loft etiquette" (safety) with students the first day of school. Having such a structure in the room is somewhat of a novelty and definitely lots of fun, but safety comes first. Talk with students about the dangers of unsafe behavior on or around the loft.

(For directions on how to build a classroom loft, see pp. 212-230.)

This L-shaped loft leaves plenty of room below for computer workspace and step-table storage and adequate room up top for a quiet reading space or even a class puppet show!

Room 6 Puppet Shows

The students in my classroom love to perform impromptu puppet shows. The railing of the loft makes a natural stage for these shows. Students write scripts and practice with the puppets during their free-choice time. During lunch recess, students set up the theater, complete with seat numbers and tickets; they create signs that they use to open and close the show; and finally, they write a "B" on the back of several show tickets. Students who choose these special tickets are invited "backstage" after the performance to meet the actors!

Step Tables

Use step tables for work areas and storage cubbies at different areas around the room. And when the class or a small group needs to gather, bring several steps together to create a two-level meeting spot. You might also use steps to create a performance area where children can elevate themselves before their audience. (For directions on how to make step tables, see pp. 210-211.)

A Peek Inside Room 6

Centers

There is much to cover in the first-grade year, and while whole-class and small-group instruction address curriculum, independent learning centers give students extra learning space. Centers are great places for:

- further exploration of a concept
- reinforcement of a specific skill
- extension activities

Multiple Intelligences

Multiple intelligences refers to the various ways people learn. Intelligences include:

- verbal-linguistic
- logical-mathematical
- visual-spatial
- bodily-kinesthetic
- musical-rhythmic
- naturalist
- interpersonal
- intrapersonal

Centers are perfect spaces to address the different ways in which students learn. For example, one of your students might learn best through discussion (verbal-linguistic), while another student may have to draw something out (visual-spatial). Author Howard Gardner began this conversation with his research about the problem-solving skills each of us uses as we acquire new knowledge. He and others explain how teachers can apply information on multiple intelligences in the classroom.

Centers and State Standards

Research your school district's state standards-based curriculum expectations. If you need to cover properties of water, for example, a center will help you accomplish this instruction, *and* allow students to have fun with hands-on activities. Centers can also reinforce a large-group lesson for smaller groups of students. Make directions for your centers that highlight what your students should do in this independent activity.

Centers may also be areas of your classroom where common curriculum items are stored. Below are different learning centers you might want to include in your classroom:

- Book Nook
- Writing Area
- Math Center
- Science Center
- Art Area

Curriculum centers like the ones above are open-ended and allow children to freely explore materials at hand. Other teachers prefer to have specific expectations (e.g., properties of water) for their centers, however. These center expectations would change once all of the children have experienced a particular material, game, or activity.

I use centers that remain consistent throughout the year but whose activities change, depending on students' developmental stages.

When creating a center, consider the following:

- Arrange center materials at student-height.
- Clearly outline your expectations for student behavior.
- Develop schedules that indicate the number of centers a child should visit in a day or a week.
- Ask children to fill out recording sheets. These sheets record students' center choices and those tasks they have performed at these areas.(See page 22 for related Q&A.)
- Allow students to make their own choices.

A good rule of thumb is to keep the management and care of centers as simple as possible. If it becomes too burdensome for either you or the students, no one will want to visit them.

Question & Answer

How often should I change my centers?

You can change your centers
- once a week
- once students have finished a specific activity
- at the end of the year

Print Hunt

A Peek Inside Room 6

"Print Hunt" is an activity and center rolled into one! Print Hunt requires students to utilize print on your classroom walls. The center remains the same, but the print on the classroom walls (e.g., project work, poetry, oral news shares, theme vocabulary, word walls, etc.) changes during the year, thereby allowing students to constantly reinforce skills, but with timely new material.

In Room 6, students may participate in a "print hunt" during their free-choice time. I usually limit the number of students who can participate by placing between one and five (you may use more or less) Finger Pointers in a container at the center.

Finger Pointers are stuffed cloth gloves fastened securely at the end of a wooded dowel; they resemble a hand, pointer finger extended. Finger Pointers are 24" long, are available in vibrant colors, and are decorated with sparkly rings and wristbands! Teachers can even attach an old-fashioned bicycle bell to "ring" for students' attention.

Students take a Finger Pointer from the canister, and alone or with a partner they walk around the room, quietly reading the print on the walls.

Question & Answer

How do I manage centers?

To help keep you and your students organized, and to utilize centers effectively, build a center time into your weekly schedule. If you decide to assign a specific number of centers to your students each week, then students may select the centers in the order they prefer. Students know they must finish the tasks at the required centers by the end of the week and that after they complete required centers, they can make free choices.

How do students know if a center is full? One option is to write each student's name on a Popsicle stick. Keep the Popsicle stick canister in a convenient location. Students can take the Popsicle stick with their name and place it in the learning center jar. When there are four sticks in the center's cup, for example, then no one else can join that center. These are good visuals for young learners, too. Another option is to have students count to four.

If you decide to assign groups of students to specific centers, create icons that represent each center, laminate the icons, stick Velcro on the back of each one, and place on a "work board," as discussed by Irene Fountas and Gay Su Pinnell in their book *Guided Reading:Good First Teaching for All Children*. List student groups at the top of the board and move icons each day by attaching the back of the center icon to the Velcro positioned underneath the group names.

Recording sheets can also be used. These work better with older students, however, as first graders are still developing their fine-motor skills. If you decide to use a recording sheet, devise one in which students simply write their name, the date, and the center they attended. Have students place a check next to the skill or activity they completed. Once students have filled out their recording sheets, they may place them in a designated area. Some teachers, for example, ask students to place such sheets in "weekly" or "daily" work folders.

Our Mail Center

Skills

proper letter formation

spelling/encoding

writing

punctuation

calendar and date writing

proofreading

theme content: "learning check-in"

friendly letter format (i.e., letter that contains date, greeting, body text, and closing)

writing with a purpose

Materials

old stationery/cards/postcards (See page 26 for postcard reproducible.)

envelopes, all sizes

construction paper

pens, markers, pencils

stencils

stamps for creating personal stationery

postal mailbox for outgoing mail

mail cubbies for classmates

computer with spell check

dictionary

    child-created with words students know how to spell

    rebus

    class-made, theme-related

    professionally published for elementary students

    electronic spell checker

poster with example of friendly letter format

chart with friendly letter "vocabulary" written on it, which can be added to throughout
    the year (e.g., dear, yours, truly, friend, sincerely, etc.)

word wall

Personnel

    Mail person: Delivers outgoing mail and classroom mail. (This job may change weekly or monthly in order to give each student in your classroom a turn.)

Activity

Children use the center to write notes and letters to people at home, in the classroom, or in other classrooms or offices within the school. They may design their own stationery or choose from available cards and papers. Students should follow the friendly letter format, which requires a greeting and a closing in their letters. I usually teach my class how to write a friendly letter during the very first weeks of the school year by writing a class letter to someone in the school. Often we write to our school principal, introducing ourselves to him and inviting him to visit us when he has time. Students are thrilled when they receive a friendly letter response from the principal!

Expectations

Before students place mail in the mailbox, they must proof it for known spelling, punctuation, and use of capital letters. Students may proof alone or with a friend. If you decide to use this center the entire year, add skills and change activities and content focus periodically. For example, during a study of animal habitats, place a direction card at the center that asks students to design a postcard with a picture of an animal and its habitat on one side. This time their letter should include information they have learned in this animal theme-study. Children should complete this letter first before writing any other letters.

Spin-off Activity

Have your students design a class stamp. Stamps can
- be drawn or created by carving in Styrofoam or rubber, inking the surface with water-based paint (use nontoxic, water-based paint); print stamps on envelopes or postcards
- change with the theme being studied

Ask the mail carrier to date and stamp each letter as it leaves the postal area.

Name _____ Date _____

Today I: ✏️

___ wrote a letter to _____

___ wrote a postcard to _____

___ designed my own stationery

___ designed my own postcard

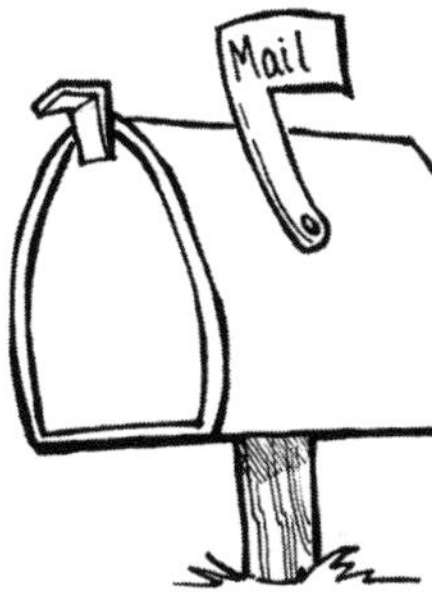

I "proofed" my writing by:

___ checking the word wall
___ asking a friend
___ sounding out my words
___ looking around for examples
___ other_____

Next time I go to the Mail Center, I want to:

_____

_____

Teacher Comments:

_____

_____

Greetings

Reproducible

CLASSROOM MANAGEMENT TIPS AND TECHNIQUES

Your classroom looks great. Your Welcome Board reaches out to the children and their parents. Your book collection is visible and well selected. Your choice of furniture and work areas clearly matches what you know about your students. Your love for math manipulatives and "found stuff" is obvious due to the choice and abundance of hands-on materials present in your classroom. Your first newsletter will go out at the end of the week. You have thought of everything...or have you?

Along with a great classroom look must come a great classroom community. It is this community, or family-like feeling, that will allow you the greatest opportunities to really work with your students as the unique individuals they are. This sense of community is taught and modeled in the very best classrooms, no matter the grade level.

What is *community*? Community is that sense of group where children learn to value one another's differences and similarities. Children within a community tend to look out for one another; they care about their classmates and their classroom environment. A community atmosphere is nonthreatening, allowing all children to do their personal best and to be appreciated for that best. Process-oriented activities (e.g., the writing process—writing a story) often take the place of more product-oriented activities in a community. After all, learning is a process, and we are all in the process together.

Building Community: Tips, Tips . . .

Help foster community with students through routines, class meetings, field trips, hands-on experiences, and flexible grouping. For example, routines, when developed with your class, give students a sense of ownership in the schedule and define specific time blocks, and a class meeting is a routine that helps children get to know one another through group discussion and interaction.

Building community, however, takes time, but this is time well spent when you consider the difficulties you may be preventing from happening during the year. Imagine not having to spend so much time on behavioral issues!

Children are less likely to misbehave, whine, and tattle when they

- feel accepted and part of the group
- see each other as real people
- own and devise the class rules for the use of class materials

Active participation in the governing and teaching processes within your classroom will decrease the number of behavioral problems. Think about the increased learning opportunities for all students when your students automatically help each other with academic tasks. The young "teachers" have an opportunity to articulate knowledge learned, while their "student" hears another person's understanding of a skill piece. This peer-to-peer instruction may be just the nudge the child needs to make that learning his/her own!

Question & Answer

Why do you say that building classroom community takes extra time?

In a teacher-directed classroom where community is not the focus, lessons are not necessarily taught with consideration to a group made up of unique individuals. Instead, the focus is curriculum content. When you build classroom community, your first focus must be the students, not the curriculum. It takes time to really get to know students as people and for them to get to know each other. Then your lessons are tailored to meet individual needs and preferences of your students.

. . . and More Tips!

Children at this age are generally egocentric and must therefore be taught the why's and how's of community. Author Martha Kaufeldt writes about the brain's development within a healthy community:

> *The brain's capabilities are enhanced by positive social interactions. One's own identity and the ability to learn are profoundly influenced by noncompetitive, interpersonal relationships and one's feeling of inclusion in a social group (1999).*

Below are some tips on how to build and maintain community with your students:

Tip #1: Take time to teach the procedures/routines of your classroom. This is time well spent!

Tip #2: Ask children to develop class rules at the beginning of the year. Rules might include:

- No put downs
- Don't interrupt unless it's an emergency
- Work together to resolve problems
- Everyone should try his/her best
- Listen actively
- Communicate ideas
- Respect differences
- Share responsibilities

You might even consider creating and acting in skits with your students that demonstrate how "breaking" classroom rules can negatively affect community. This is also a good time to teach social skills.

Tip #3: Establish a class meeting system where you and your students openly discuss both positive and negative happenings within the classroom.

Tip #4: Vary teaching methods, keeping in mind your individual learners.

Tip #5: Use different groupings for instruction.

Tip #6: Give your students real responsibilities for taking care of their classroom environment.

Tip #7: Encourage your students to contribute to the academic plan through generative curriculum building.

Tip #8: Plan times during the day for children to be social and share with one another.

Tip #9: Give your students real choices within their school day.

Tip #10: Plan ways to include your parents/family members in school learning.

Getting-to-Know-You Activities

Following are two fun getting-to-know-you activities. Try both with your class and watch your community begin to grow!

BINGO!

This is a fun getting-to-know-you activity to play with your first graders at the beginning of the year. The directions are simple:

1. With your class review all appropriate vocabulary represented on the bingo sheet (color words, clothing items, etc.)
2. Demonstrate how the game of bingo is played.
3. Have students find classmates who fit the picture clue in the squares (they should try not to interview anyone more than two times).
4. When they have found a match for a particular box, each student should introduce him/herself and make a mark of some kind in that box. When someone has marked four connected squares (across, diagonally, up, or down), s/he can yell, "Bingo!"

Bingo!

Community and Friendships Formed Through a Field Trip

One year our community-building experience happened earlier than usual. As I planned my beginning theme-related activities, I thought of the section in Lucy Calkins' book, 📖 *Living Between the Lines*, in which she discusses the importance of planning a substantial field trip for the beginning of the year and not the end. Teachers, notes Calkins, usually plan field trips for the end of the year because they feel this is the time when the teacher, students, and learning best come together. She argues, however, that this group should be brought together at the beginning of the year so that friendships, learning styles, and individual strengths and interests are formed and featured as early as possible.

Well, having just read Calkins' book, I was not about to take any chances, so I planned an early year experience for my diverse group of twenty-seven students—a full day hike to the shores of a beautiful pond located a short distance from our school. We packed hot dogs and supplies in our backpacks, and off we went.

The hike took over an hour through hill and dale . . . literally. Booker, my dog, bounded alongside us the entire trip. In retrospect, it was probably the inclusion of Booker that made this hike a real bonding experience. As Booker leaped and hugged children and periodically checked back with me, the children saw me as a real person, someone who existed in ways that were familiar to them. The school walls were gone. We joked, laughed, and allowed ourselves to get to know each other in a situation that placed us all on the same footing.

I carry a picture in my memory of my students at the end of this glorious day: some sitting together on the rug by the story chair, others nestled in the fur of a very tired but content and happy golden retriever, and still others quietly napping while waiting for the bus. When they left the classroom and headed for the buses, I heard snippets of conversations as they met up with friends from other classrooms: "What? Oh, that's Booker, Ms. T's dog. Yeah, really, her dog. He goes everywhere with us. His favorite thing to do is to give hugs, and if he slobbers on you, that means he really likes you." "Your teacher has a dog? Cool!"

Who would have thought my bouncy five-year-old golden retriever (who never quite passed his doggy obedience class) would be the key for bringing together this diverse group. But Booker did just that, and the children included him in our classroom community. They mentioned his name often, and cheers sounded happily whenever he visited. Room 6 students often asked how Booker was doing, and I gladly shared with them stories about his household antics. He became the bond around which the

children connected. They shared a common memory, something fun and different. Something (and someone) they will always remember with fondness.

The hike accomplished all that Lucy Calkins said it would. The children discovered new things about each other that would not have surfaced as quickly in the confines of a classroom. On our adventure the children saw each other as real people, kids with interests similar to their own. I remember watching one student in particular, who was usually boisterous and energetic, carefully hold trailside branches for another classmate. I could hear, "Thank you" and "No, that's okay" voiced repeatedly throughout the day. I later whispered to this student, "I really like how you are looking out for Arthur. What a good friend you are." He looked back at me and said, "You know, Ms. T., Arthur is really hard to get to like. But once you get to know him, he's okay!" I smiled, thinking back on my first experiences with that child and how I had had the very same thought!

A giant "puff ball" mushroom discovered on our hike.

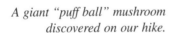

Hiking to Colchester Pond.

Routines

Classroom routines are a must. Without routines, teachers would have to invent each time block every day, classrooms would be very teacher-directed, and teachers would "own" processes in the room. The children could guess, but they would never be sure about what was going to happen next. This type of teaching style is much less comfortable for both the teacher and the students. The teacher is always "on" and in control of all the movement, materials, and learning patterns. I have to admit, my first classroom included several of these characteristics. What I remember most from that year was the feeling of being tired all the time. Well, no wonder—everything constantly revolved around me! My students learned, but they did not develop that nurturing, caring component on which I have come to depend.

Classroom routines allow you to
- hand over some of the ownership of the day to your students
- help make sense of the tasks at hand
- give students a feeling of empowerment in connection with their learning (This actually boosts their learning ever higher!)

Like adults, children need to feel part of the process.

Time Blocks

Take time to discuss and devise steps for routines and time blocks with your students, and then teach basic time-block procedures. When you work with students to design the structure and expectations for each block, whether it be reading, theme activities, etc., you give them ownership of their behavior and classroom expectations.

I suggest you and your students start the year off by designing and learning one or two time blocks within the first week. In Room 6 we
- discuss expectations
- practice the time block
- discuss the routine
- set the routine to paper
- hang the routine in the room

I almost always use a circular graphic to show students how the routine is continual. Adjustments, of course, are inevitably made as the year progresses, but once you establish and write down the routine, it becomes an expectation. By hanging the routine on the wall, you have created a graphic organizer for the students, yourself, instructional assistants, and parents. With the routine now in place, the children are in charge of the activity, and you can step off center stage and have time for small-group or one-on-one instruction, or observation time. (See page 34 for a sample routine.)

Question & Answer

What, exactly, is a routine?

A routine takes a behavior, sequences the steps needed to achieve the behavior, and reinforces those steps through repetition. You probably have a morning routine in your home. When the routine is in place, there is less chaos. When no routine is in place . . . well, you know the rest of the story!

Is it really important to give students choices?

Choice, however small, helps students realize their empowerment in the real day-to-day workings of the classroom. During reading time, for example, I reinforce the fact that even my beginning readers can make good reading choices based on what they know about themselves as readers.

The students are now making choices within the time block, and I am free to add in my other instructional components. I devise small, flexible groups around specific text levels, or I assign specific activities. When a group finishes, they can resume their work on the Reading Time Routine. Meanwhile, the rest of the class continues their independent reading assignments. No one is waiting for me, and I am not waiting for them.

A Peek Inside Room 6

Free-Choice Time:

Room 6 students begin most days with "Free-Choice Time." As students walk in the classroom door, the very first activity they choose to participate in is up to them. By giving the class this freedom, I am showing them that their choice is valuable. Placing students in control of this particular time block was a difficult decision; after all, this first hour is prime teaching time. When I considered the benefits gained from allowing students this choice, however, I realized that, for me, this was the best possible method of operation.

Share materials
Draw a picture (use words, too)
Snack
Science lesson
Write a book
Write a letter; mail it
Read a book
Computers
Free Choice Time
Math facts
Exercise bike
Play Abalone™
Play a game with a puppet
Loft—8 people Quiet
Work on individual goals
Create a puppet show
Write a song
Word cards
Building materials: Legos, blocks
Notebook
Board games
Games
Write a story

Now, do understand, the fact that I give them choice does not imply that chaos is the rule. The class and I set clear guidelines. Once students have decided how they would like to use their time (and they often decide long before they step into the classroom on any particular day), they get right down to business, and therefore, we waste very little time.

During Free-Choice Time students become involved in any one of our daily activities, and it is interesting to note that students often choose the same activities/projects I would have chosen for them—writers write, beginning readers practice reading, mathematicians explore new and old materials, readers read, and computer buffs try out new programs. You will hear an audible hum in the room, and you will feel a positive charge in the air, which is alive with each student's enthusiasm. The room is not quiet, but it is not noisy, either. Students are engaged and excited.

Reading Time Routine

A Peek Inside Room 6

The Reading Time Routine time block
- incorporates an academic block
- allows the children to choose their reading materials
- gives me a consistent system for periodically conferencing with them
- provides quality time for small-group instructional meetings

Take a look at the Reading Time Routine, then read the explanation for each step (see page 36).

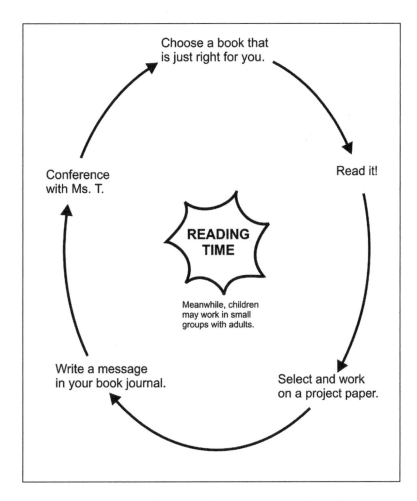

This Reading Time Routine is exceedingly simple. I have found that oftentimes "less is best." (See page 37 for an example of a modified Reading Time Routine.)

A Peek Inside Room 6

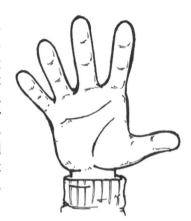

Choose a book that is just right for you: I teach students how to select books that fall into their instructional reading range, that is, books that are challenging but not too difficult. The "5- finger rule" is the easiest and best strategy to teach each student how to choose a book that is right for him/her. To apply the 5-finger rule, ask each student to pick out a book and start reading. Each time s/he makes a miscue, s/he should hold up one finger. If the student has five fingers up, that means the book is probably too hard for the student, and s/he should look for another book.

Read it! Student reads the entire book.

Select and work on a project paper: In my room I have several pocket folders filled with book projects. These are simple comprehension worksheets that require students to record information about the book s/he has just read. Book projects should take five to ten minutes to complete.

Write a message in your book journal: Each child has a book journal in which s/he writes a letter—in friendly letter format—about the book. His/her letter might be about a favorite part, a funny riddle, and/or a picture about the story.

Conference with Ms. T: Once a student finishes a book, s/he signs his/her name to a dry-erase board labeled "Reading Time Routine Conferences." I check the board frequently and conference with the student whose name appears next on the list. If I am working with a group, this student knows to begin the cycle again with another book. This allows me to control how many conferences I hold and with which students I meet each week.

At the conference the student and I discuss the book, this student reads a section to me, and we discuss the next book s/he has chosen. This is a perfect time to gather conference notes and assessment pieces. I also collect the journal entry and the book project, respond to both, then return each to the student.

This routine allows me to develop an organized academic block, allows students to choose their reading material, and provides me with a consistent system for periodically checking in with them via the conference format. It also helps reinforce that even my beginning readers can make good reading choices based on what they know about themselves as readers. Having students in charge of this portion of the time block allows me more quality time for small-group instruction.

Now, look at a modified version of the Reading Time Routine (see page 37). Note the various components I have added.

Status of the Class: I use this "Status of the Class" form to start each reading period. I call students together and ask them what book they are reading and if I have met with them about this book yet. "Status of the Class" provides me with a daily visual reminder as to whom I may need to meet with for a conference, and it helps the children reevaluate the status of their book. (For more information on Status of the Class, see page 39.)

Children may practice sight vocabulary: I have written the Dolch Sight Words—the 220 most frequently found words—on flash cards, which I have grouped into sets of ten. Children may practice these words with an assistant or with other students. I hang these same words on our class word wall. (See page 77 for the Dolch Sight-Word List.)

Special education teacher reads with individual students: I require all support services to be administered *in* the classroom. For example, a Title I teacher might do guided reading with a student in the classroom during our reading time block.

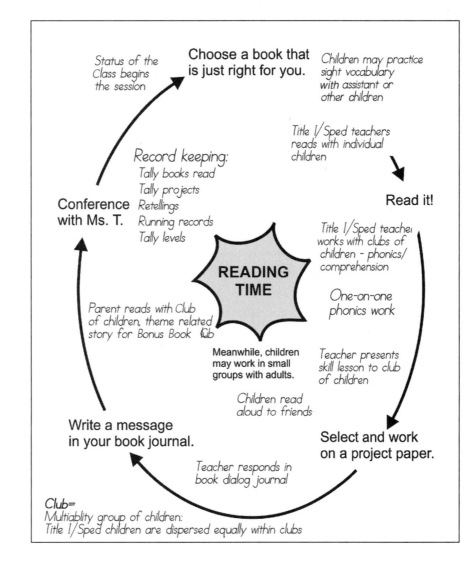

Modified version of the Reading Time Routine

Status of the Class begins the session

Choose a book that is just right for you.

Children may practice sight vocabulary with assistant or other children

Title I/Sped teachers reads with individual children

Read it!

Record keeping:
Tally books read
Tally projects
Retellings
Running records
Tally levels

Conference with Ms. T.

READING TIME

Title I/Sped teacher works with clubs of children - phonics/comprehension

One-on-one phonics work

Parent reads with Club of children, theme related story for Bonus Book Club

Meanwhile, children may work in small groups with adults.

Teacher presents skill lesson to club of children

Children read aloud to friends

Write a message in your book journal.

Select and work on a project paper.

Teacher responds in book dialog journal

Club=
Multiablity group of children:
Title I/Sped children are dispersed equally within clubs

A Peek Inside Room 6

Title I/special education teacher works with clubs of children: Special education and Title I students are dispersed equally throughout clubs. Support teachers address phonics and other reading skills with all students, while keeping in mind each student's reading level and abilities. 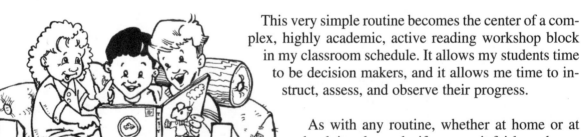 Dr. Margaret Allen's phonics books offer terrific games and activities, and Yvette Zgonc's book, *Sounds in Action*, provides fun activities and assessments that help assess phonological awareness.

One-on-one phonics work: One-on-one phonics work is done best orally with young readers. A parent, volunteer, or instructional assistant can work on phonics skills with one student at a time. This adult may use a published phonics program such as *Explode the Code* (series), by Nancy Hall and Rena Price, or *Spelling Through Phonics*, by Marlene J. and Robert A. McCracken, but all work must be done out loud, that is, orally. This is not a time for "seat work."

Teacher presents skill lesson to a club of children: Teach a skill lesson to a small club of students.

Children read aloud to friends: Students share their books with others in the room as they "master" reading the text.

Teacher responds in book dialog journal: I write a book-related message back to each child in his/her journal.

Parent reads a Bonus Book Club book with a student group: This is a fun and easy activity to have ready for a drop-in parent volunteer. Volunteer reads a theme-related story to a group of students. The time spent reading is recorded and added to each student's at-home reading time. (See Chapter 7 for more information on the Book Club and the Bonus Book Club.)

Record-keeping: Tally books read, projects, retellings, running records, and levels. During each conference I keep track of information in short cryptic notes. I may also do a running record as the child reads aloud. This information is stored in each child's section of my teacher's portfolio. (See Chapter 4 for more information on record-keeping.)

Note: A **club** is a work group that is not designated by ability. These clubs can be very diverse in their makeup.

This very simple routine becomes the center of a complex, highly academic, active reading workshop block in my classroom schedule. It allows my students time to be decision makers, and it allows me time to instruct, assess, and observe their progress.

As with any routine, whether at home or at school, it only works if you use it fairly and consistently. Children will need time to learn and practice this routine. Remember, they were not born understanding reading workshop, but in time such routines will become automatic.

Status of the Class

Routines work best when everyone knows where they are on the routine as soon as the time block begins. My favorite start-up tool is Nancie Atwell's "Status of the Class," which may be found in her book, 📖 *In the Middle: New Understandings About Writing, Reading, and Learning*. Atwell used this form in her process-writing classroom with middle school students, but it works just as well for reading, writing, math, and spelling workshop times for younger students. (See page 41 for Status of the Class reproducible.)

My Status of the Class form, inspired by and adopted from Nancie Atwell's work, fits well into all areas of the curriculum. The coding symbols appear at the bottom of the form. I use different clipboards for each workshop time.

STATUS OF THE CLASS   (READING/WRITING/MATH)

Date 4|17

Name	Monday	Tuesday	Wednesday	Thursday	Friday
Aaron	The Meanies ↗	Ⓒ	→ Brown Bear Brown Bear		
Justine	Give a Mouse a Cookie ↗	Ⓒ	→ Give a moose a Muffin		
Matt	Brown Bear Ⓒ	→ Polar Polar Bear			
Jesse	Trucks	Ⓒ → Give a pig a Pancake			
Kari	Catwings ↗	Ⓒ → Catwings Returns			
Laura	The Jolly Roger ↗				
Greg	6 Snowy Sheep Ⓒ	6 sleepy Sheep			
Scott	Very Hungry Caterpillar Ⓒ	The Witch Nextdoor			
Anne	Heckedy Peg ↗	Ⓒ →			
Nina	My Father's Dragon ↗				
Ross	The Napping House ↗	Ⓒ → House that Jack Built			
Drew	Cream of Creature ↗				
Rebekah	The Tiny Seed Ⓒ	Grouchy Ladybug			
Cindy	Clifford Red the Big Dog ↗				
Kyle	We share Everything ↗	Ⓒ → The Tiny Seed			
Samantha	6 sleepy Sheep Ⓒ	6 snowy Sheep			
Ethan	I was so mad ↗				
Carlos	Little Critters Ⓒ	→ Dan the Flying Man			
Meiyi	Paper bag Princess ↗	Ⓒ	Principal's new Clothes		
Heather	Just Go To Bed Ⓒ	→ Just Me and my Grandpa			
Karl	10 Sly Piranhas ↗ Ⓒ	Companies Coming			

Reading	**Writing**		**Math**
New Title = Title	New Story = Title	Editing Conference = E	Games = G
Ongoing = →	Ongoing = →	Illustrating = Pub.	Journal = J
Conference = C	Peer Conference = P		Papers = P
	Content Conference = C		Conference = C

This Status of the Class form was filled out for a Monday-Tuesday block. The books in Wednesday's block were shared with me at the Tuesday conference, so I jotted them down as known information.

When I do "Status" on Wednesdays I will acknowledge those books aloud. A blank indicates the student had the conference but still needs to find a next book.

Quiet Transitions

Activities such as Status of the Class help transition students from one setting to another. Transitions also allow the teacher to

- gather information
- remind students of their tasks
- dismiss students from the rug, or another area in small groups, making the transition much more orderly

Assign one of your students to select background music for workshop time (this could be a class job). This student knows s/he can play music that has a quiet hum to it—not too loud, but not too soft—and that s/he can choose from the variety of tapes or CD's present in the classroom. Environmental-sounds tapes or CD's are often a good choice, as they are gentle and soothing. The student knows not to play any music until the sound level in the room is just right.

Signal the end of a workshop time with the ringing of a kitchen timer. Over the years I have discovered that when I set the timer for five minutes before the end of the time block, the students hear that audible ticking and use it as their five-minute warning that workshop time is almost over. Students begin to finish their work, and when the timer rings, it usually takes less than three minutes to put away individual items and clean up the room.

At this time in Room 6, I head to my story chair at the rug area, and as students finish picking up, they gather with me on the rug. Because the students know the routine so well, I have not had to say a single word this entire time!

At the class meeting area, discuss workshop time with students:

- How did it go?
- Would anyone like to share what s/he accomplished today?
- Is there anything we need to improve?

The children love to share and discuss this time period. And often it is a student who addresses a need or a problem, and, along with others, brainstorms a solution. Because they are so fully invested in how the classroom works, you will find that discipline becomes less of an issue.

Class Meetings

Your class, as with any community, needs many opportunities to express new ideas, feelings, and concerns. It is this exchange that will keep your classroom community vital, enlivened, and healthy.

A class meeting is just that: a meeting of class members. It doesn't need to be fancy, but it does need to happen. I suggest your class meet at least once a week in a comfortable area of the room where everyone, including you, sits in the circle. In Room 6, the day and time are designed around the needs of the class.

The routine that starts Room 6 class meetings is the "Good Stuff/Bad Stuff Cycle."

To create:
- Draw a large circle in the middle of an oversized blank piece of construction paper.
- Within the circle, write the words: Good Stuff/Bad Stuff. Explain to students that if they have something they need to share—good or bad—they can sign their names to the paper. You may also sign your name on this paper when you have an issue to share.
- Post it on the wall in a visible place in your classroom.

If the list is long, it alerts the class to schedule a meeting as soon as possible.

I suggest you also create with students expectations for your conversations. Keep the conversations nameless—children learn quickly to describe the behavior when they are not allowed to name names, and therefore conversations tend to remain more neutral. You might be surprised to find that the student who offers the solution to the difficulty is actually the same student who started the problem. This nameless telling allows the student to tell his/her side of the problem without losing face.

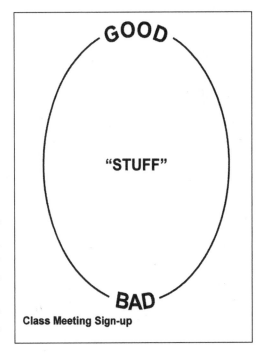

Class Meeting Sign-up

Question & Answer

Is it really that important that the class sit in a circle for a class meeting?

The circle is the best shape, even if it means moving some furniture around. It's important for the students and the teacher to be able to see one another when they are speaking. The circle also helps everyone feel included, whether they speak at the meeting or not.

The class meeting time has its own set of routines that the students and teacher design at the first meeting of the year.

As with all routines, visit the routine again and again, giving the class the practice needed for this time block in which potentially emotional subjects, such as behavior, are discussed.

What do you mean by the term "losing face"?

I have found when a child is expressing his/her behavior in ways I would like to discourage, it is better to give him/her the chance to turn it around him/herself, thereby not "losing face" with his/her peers.

Too often we back kids into a corner for which their only recourse is to admit defeat or try to "win." I try to offer students behavioral choices at times like these so they can take ownership of their own actions.

Behavior Choices

The following three stories have to do with respecting children and letting them know how you honestly feel. These stories also have to do with letting students make their own choices when it comes to their behavior—in other words, letting them *own* their behavior. As teachers, it's easy to *tell* students what to do, but by letting them decide, the message becomes much stronger, and you are no longer *forcing* them to do something; instead, you are giving them options from which to choose, and that makes a difference. As you will see, these three boys needed to learn how to become part of and function with a group—not in charge of it, not isolated from it. They needed to be *in* the room so they could observe the appropriate behavior being modeled for them. *

Michael

Early one fall I noticed one of the little guys in my class behaving quite differently from the other students. Whenever things were not going well for Michael he would hide under a table and refuse to come out—no matter how much coaxing I did. This was his escape from work he did not want to do, from kids who were teasing him, and even from bad feelings about circumstances outside school. I knew immediately this behavior was going to alienate him from his classmates and would impede the growth of what I hoped to become an accepting community of learners.

I decided I would talk with Michael about this behavior on a "good" day—before he began retreating under furniture. I wanted him to know there were other ways he could let me know he was upset. As we talked, I showed him a small stuffed animal I had brought from home. It was a hedgehog who closely resembled the real hedgehog that lived at my house, Amaryllis. The children in the class loved hearing stories about Amaryllis, and I was counting on Michael's interest, too. I let Michael hold the hedgehog, and together we decided that whenever he was feeling low, he could get the hedgehog and hold it. This would give me a signal that he was not feeling good about himself at that moment, and I would not ask him to do anything he could not handle while he was holding the stuffed toy. We chose a secret area in the room for the hedgehog that only he and I knew about. We were ready to give it a try.

For several weeks, Michael retrieved the hedgehog frequently, making sure I noticed his actions each time. I gave him a wink and a "thumbs up" every time he did this. It was not long before he retrieved the hedgehog less often, and eventually he not only stopped hiding under furniture, but he stopped getting the hedgehog, too!

Students' real names are not used in these recollections.

A Peek Inside Room 6

Jasper

One May I offered to have a student be moved into my room, as he and his teacher were constantly at odds with one another. The situation was emotional for both, and I knew the raised voices and misbehavior was unhealthy for everyone.

When Jasper arrived in Room 6 he manifested himself as a very shy and insecure little boy. He was not loud, he was not defiant, but he was on edge and kept watching his new class members and me at all times. The classroom Jasper had recently left was a "sit-in-your-seat" type of room, but ours was much more open, and the children were used to making choices about their materials and even where they sat. Jasper was wide-eyed with all of this movement. We shared stories of the classroom with him. We taught him games to play during math time. We involved him in everything we could possibly think of that would help him transition into this new environment. He joined in, but he remained virtually silent.

After a few weeks in the classroom, Jasper started calling attention to himself by making noises and trying to distract me. The result of this behavior in his former classroom was negative. In our classroom, however, we first tried to ignore his actions, and if that didn't work, we would quietly speak to him. One time, for example, I reached over and gently placed my hand on his arm and said, "I know you are new in our classroom, but you need to know that we don't make those sounds at the rug area. So, if you want to stay at the rug with us, you will need to stop. If you would rather continue, you can, but you will have to move to another area in the room." Well, Jasper stopped making those noises immediately. He wanted to stay with the group. At other times I could see him trying out some of his "best" behaviors during independent work times. He found out quickly that no one paid much attention to him—they had activities they had chosen and were engrossed in, so he discontinued his behavior.

Because Jasper was not attracting the negative attention, as he had done in his former classroom, his behavior improved, and our class had a chance to grow into the community it was meant to be.

A Peek Inside Room 6

Jacob

My last story involves a child who had completely alienated himself from his classroom by the second week of October. Everyone in school knew it, as Jacob spent a substantial amount of his school day in "time out," located in the hallway. An adult was even assigned to "watch" Jacob, a loud, belligerent, and distant first grader. I had tried to engage him in a conversation on several occasions, only to be spit on or ignored!

Despite Jacob's behavior, I decided to volunteer Room 6 as his new classroom. My students were getting along well, our community was built, and I was sure the students could accept a newcomer, one who would need everyone's support. So it was decided—Wednesday afternoon at 1:00 p.m., Jacob would visit Room 6. He would do this for the remainder of the week and then join us full time the following Monday.

In order to prepare for Jacob's arrival, we sat down together to decide what we should do with Jacob first. We didn't want to overwhelm him, so we decided the class should be involved in a "free-choice time" so Jacob could see the fun games and activities available for students to participate in. A great plan, right? Well, when 1:00 p.m. arrived, Jacob appeared at the door to Room 6. There must have been five adults accompanying him (including his mother), and I could tell immediately that things were going poorly: two adults were holding Jacob's arms and pulling him through the door. But Jacob was going nowhere. As soon as those adults started forcing him into the classroom, Jacob started resisting by grasping both sides of the door with his hands and jamming his legs into either side of the frame. It looked as if no one was going to budge him. But I knew I couldn't let *this* be the students' first impression of Jacob, and I was going to have to intervene. I kneeled in front of this angry little boy—at eye level—and began talking to him. I told him that most kids liked this room, and as I took his hand, I asked him if he knew that we had an iguana in the classroom. He said he didn't know that, so I asked him if he wanted to see it, and he did. So off we went!

Jacob never "visited" again. He became a permanent member of our classroom the very moment he took my hand. He had been diagnosed as "oppositional defiant," yet those adults were trying with all their might to force him through the door. I, along with my class, however, *invited* Jacob—a big difference.

In Room 6, Jacob had much to learn—after all, he had spent most of his time in the hallway, so he had never learned how to work within a group setting. To me, this was the most important skill he *should* learn. The academics would come, but this was a priority.

A Peek Inside Room 6

Jacob was wide-eyed as he looked around the room at the other students. He did a lot of watching at first, which was fine with me; he needed time to acclimate himself. Eventually, he started to demonstrate some of his former behaviors, such as spitting, but the students told him immediately that if he did that again they wouldn't play with him. Jacob stopped spitting. At the rug area he began making noises and touching other people. I explained our rule: "We don't do that at the rug area. You can stop the behavior and stay here, or you can choose to continue at a table away from the rug area." When I asked Jacob what his choice was, he replied, "I want to stay here." "Great," I said. "I was hoping you would."

Jacob was never sent out of the room. He was always given responsibility for his own behavior, and the consequences for his behavior were logical: "If I want friends, I can't spit on them."

Students of all ages need time to sit down, share ideas, make decisions, plan events, and solve problems. Being actively involved in this process gives them a stronger commitment to the class structures. They learn problem-solving and conflict-resolution skills. In addition, they learn to listen, consider, and respond to other students' perspectives.

I remain a member of the circle at all times, but I am not usually the person who "runs" the meetings. Often a child takes the circle chart and starts the process. From that point the process really keeps the circle meeting on track. However, because your meeting time is limited, assign a timekeeper.

With the consistent use of class meetings, routines, and choice, I find little need for extrinsic reward systems. You, too, will find that your classroom will grow into a caring community of learners.

Classroom Schedules

Your schedule should match your instructional goals for your class. It will need to be changed often, however, as first graders become more independent and comfortable within the school environment and with their curriculum studies.

When designing your classroom schedule, write in the "have-to's" first. "Have-to's" are those time blocks over which you might have little control, such as physical education, art, music, library time, lunch, and recess. I know I want support services to be in the room during a similar time block. That is, my Title I reading teacher would work with students during a language arts time block—not during a math or science block.

Here's where people coordination is a must! I have found that if I place some of my instructional time blocks in the least popular times (i.e., times during which most teachers *are not* instructing their class in a certain curriculum area), I am more apt to be able to schedule special educators and remedial support staff. I have been known to completely change my schedule based on the schedules of these folks so that students are not pulled out of the room for work in a curriculum area different from the one on which the entire class is working.

Certified teachers who work within my classroom plan their own lessons, but we try to look at it as a combined effort, usually setting up a weekly meeting to discuss how everything is going and if any changes need to be made.

To create a schedule:
- Begin with an empty grid. (See p.49.)
- Fill in the "have-to's" first.
- Consider support-service time next.
- Finish with class routines and instructional time. (Consider if you want to build a theme day or a center day into your schedule.)

Use the grid to fit the pieces of your schedule together. (It may take more than one try!) Use your finished copy as the basis for your classroom plans. Copy multiple schedules each week, then jot down your lesson plans in the blocks, and off you go! Remember, you can do this by hand or you can type your plans on the computer, whichever saves you the most time! Give copies of your weekly schedule to administrators, specialists, and parents, and always keep one handy in case you require a substitute. (See page 59 for more information on lesson plans.)

Room 6 Classroom Schedule
Free-Choice Time = a center time. Science and social studies concepts are integrated within all of our time blocks. At times we will take whole days or even weeks to explore these concepts in depth.

Grade 1	Monday	Tuesday	Wednesday	Thursday	Friday
8:40 – 9:15	←	FREE	CHOICE	TIME	→
9:15 – 9:40	News Share Today's News Secret Message Proofreading	Poetry	News Share	Poetry	News Share
9:40 – 10:25	Key Word Time Get new words Write/illustrate Word analysis	Music	Physical Education	Library	Math
10:30 – 10:50	Recess	Recess	Recess	Recess	Recess
10:50 – 11:55	Reading Club Status of Class Self-selected Reading Conferences Instructional groups	Reading Club	Writing Club Status of the Class Independent Writing Conferences Instructional groups	Writing Club	Reading/Writing Club
12:00 – 12:40	Lunch/Recess	Lunch/Recess	Lunch/Recess	Lunch/Recess	Lunch/Recess
12:40 – 12:50	Traveling Books	Traveling Books	Art	Traveling Books	Traveling Books
12:50 – 1:15	Story Time	Story Time		Story Time	Story Time
1:15 – 1:30	Silent Reading	Silent Reading		Silent Reading	Silent Reading
1:30 – 2:15	Math	Math		Math	Math
2:15 – 3:00	Spelling Workshop — Word Wall Work	Spelling Workshop — Word Wall Work		Spelling Workshop— Word Wall Work	Physical Education

Hot lunch = $1.25; choc/juice = $.35; reg., skim milk = $.25. Lunch money is collected and recorded on the first day of the week. Dismissal begins at 3:00 PM

Class Schedule

	Monday	Tuesday	Wednesday	Thursday	Friday
TIME:					
	LUNCH	LUNCH	LUNCH	LUNCH	LUNCH
Dismissal:					

Reproducible

Instruction

With your classroom schedule organized, the children functioning as a community, and students making good choices within their classroom routines, consider how you would like to deliver instruction. In Room 6, instruction comes in many different forms. At times, whole-group instruction is the best mode for certain skill discussions; at other times, I find that teaching to smaller heterogeneous groups works better. Still, there are times when a smaller group is best taught if it is characterized by its similarity of skill-level attainment. I always save a place for those one-on-one instructional moments.

Whole-group instruction works best when you are
- introducing new concepts
- sharing about one another in the lesson
- using an active mode of instruction
- using story to engage students
- using theme to integrate subject areas

Small-group instruction works best when you are
- reinforcing skill instruction
- guiding new instruction
- looking for cooperative outcomes

One-on-one instruction works best when you are
- reinforcing learned skills
- noting individual skill attainment
- engaging in conversation

Consider and incorporate all three groupings into your instruction.

Teaching Activity	Whole Group	Small Group	Individual Student
Language Arts			
Status of the Class	Daily		
Self-Selected Reading			As Needed
Mini-Lessons	As Needed	2-3 Times Weekly	As Needed
Conferences			As Needed
Today's News	3 Times Weekly		
Poetry	2 Times Weekly		
Minimal-Cues Messages	3 Times Weekly		
Proofreading Messages	3 Times Weekly		
Spelling Counts			1 Time Weekly
Guided Reading Group		2 Times Weekly	2 Times Weekly
Literature Circles		As Needed	
Conversation Journals			Daily
Read Aloud Chapt. Books	Daily		
Author's Chair	As Needed		
Key Word Time	1 Time Weekly	As Needed	1 Time Weekly
Mathematics			
Status of the Class	Daily		
Self-Selected Activities			As Needed
Journal			1 Time Weekly
Mini-Lessons	As Needed	2-3 Times Weekly	As Needed
Problem-Solving	As Needed	1 Time Weekly	As Needed
Drill Sheets			1 Time Weekly
Science/Social Studies			
Thematic Studies			
New Information	3 Times Weekly		
Independent Study			As Needed
Projects	As Needed	As Needed	As Needed
Field Trips	As Needed		
Read Aloud	Daily	1 Time/Week	
Videos	As Needed		
Guest Speakers	As Needed		
Research		1 Marking Period	
Art Connections	1 Time Weekly		
Music Connections	1 Time Weekly		
PE Connections	2 Times Weekly		
Technology Connections	As Needed	1 Time Weekly	As Needed

Room 6 Sample Instruction Plan

TIME MANAGEMENT TIPS

Do you ever feel like there's not enough of you to go around? Part of being a good teacher is understanding when it is okay to give yourself permission to invite others (parents, colleagues, and even students) to take over some classroom responsibilities. When you delegate certain responsibilities or find faster, more convenient, and better means by which to complete tasks, you will feel more relaxed around your students and will accomplish more in those areas over which you retain control. Best of all, you will empower others in the classroom, resulting in bigger and better performances from everyone, including yourself.

A good rule of thumb: Consider which tasks monopolize the greatest amount of your time. Are they teaching/professional activities, or are they clerical, nonprofessional duties? True, we are expected to perform lots of tasks (with students close at our side), but remember, don't hesitate to delegate some of these duties. You might even consider transferring responsibility for certain classroom jobs for the entire year (e.g., creating display bulletin boards, publishing the class newsletter, etc.).

Here's what to do:
- Map out your own list of daily/weekly responsibilities. (See page 53 for list reproducible.)
- Identify nonprofessional tasks.
- Ask a parent or community volunteer to take ownership of one or more of these activities.
- Invite students to help out in certain areas.
- Review your forms and worksheets.
- Identify open-ended forms and worksheets already available so you are not always starting from scratch.

Daily/Weekly Professional Responsibilities	Daily/Weekly Nonprofessional Responsibilities
• Write individual notes to parents • Write letters to class to inform them of upcoming events • Plan lessons: theme/academic areas • Administer ongoing assessments • Meet with other professionals in the building to discuss instructional program • Meet with paraprofessionals who work in the classroom • Meet with parents about student performance • Attend faculty meetings • Teach whole-group lessons, e.g., Today's News, Secret Message, Read Aloud, etc. • Conduct small-group lessons • Conduct one-on-one lessons in conferences • Chat with children/parents • Model lessons • Create and update bulletin boards that display active learning • Read/research for lesson planning • Complete committee work/attendance • Create worksheets/games/activities that complement learning • Create and update substitute plans	• Take attendance • Take lunch count • Fulfill recess duty • Photocopy papers • Fulfill bus duty • Keep class progress charts up-to-date • Create display bulletin boards • Complete book orders • Collate field trip information • Call parents for donations of time or help • Work with students on flash cards, timed math tests, class newsletter, and spelling check-ins • Pick up room/materials • Type student stories • Bind student-published books • Put together file folder games, etc. • Pass out papers

Sample Professional/Nonprofessional Responsibilities

Leave Plenty of Time!

As with any group of first graders, leave plenty of time at the end of each work period to gather work, put away materials, put on coats and mittens, and pass papers back. Getting into and out of snowsuits, hats, and boots during a Vermont winter, for example, can be a whole-day event! During these cold and snowy months, I end my last time block of the day ten minutes earlier than I do during the fall and spring.

Home-School Folders

Passing back papers can also take time. Consider using a home-school folder system in which corrected papers or information that parents need to read are filed into each student's folder (earlier in the day) by a class volunteer or student helper. Now the only item you need to pass out at the end of the day are students' folders! Students can also use these folders to transport information from their parents to their teacher.

Remember that your students can help with lots of tasks throughout the school day. Stacking chairs, sorting books and papers, and cleaning up the room and hallway are all easy, but necessary, jobs. Your first graders will enjoy the responsibility, and you will enjoy having a little extra time for something else.

Daily/Weekly Professional Responsibilities	Daily/Weekly Nonprofessional Responsibilities

Reproducible

A Peek Inside Room 6

Here is an example of my school day:

7:45 a.m.
- Arrive at school
- Unpack work completed at home
- Distribute conversation notebooks
- Place corrected work in "home" box. At the end of the day, pass corrected work (stored in this box) back to students so they can bring it home.
- Check mailbox
- Complete any work needed for the school office or for the start of the school day

	MONDAY
8:40 - 9:15	**Free-Choice Time**
9:15 - 9:40	**News Share**
	•Today's News
	• Secret message
	• Proofreading
9:40 - 10:25	**Keyword Time**
	• Identify new words
	• Write/illustrate
	• Word analysis
10:30 - 10:50	**Recess**
10:50 - 11:55	**Reading Club**
	• Status of the Class
	• Self-selected reading
	• Conferences
	• Instructional groups
12:00 - 12:40	**Lunch**
12:40 - 12:50	**Traveling Books**
12:50 - 1:15	**Story Time**
1:15 - 1:30	**Silent Reading**
1:30 - 2:15	**Math**
2:15 - 3:00	**Spelling Workshop**

3:00 p.m.
- Children dress for home
- Pass out papers
- Wait for buses
- Stack chairs
- Pick up classroom

3:20 p.m.
- Gather papers/notebooks that need correcting or a written response
- Consider plans for tomorrow; make changes where necessary
- Write in conversation notebooks, taking note of individual writing/spelling patterns
- File anecdotal records and conference notes
- Prepare materials
- Meet with colleagues/parents/administrators/committees

4:30 p.m.
- Leave for home with papers and other school-related tasks to complete

At home
- Write in journals
- Correct work
- Prepare new theme-related lessons
- Write letter to parents about Room 6 news and events

Wanted: Classroom Volunteers!

Now that you have a list of those tasks with which you could use assistance, start calling for help! Begin by sending home a letter to parents at the beginning of the year that lists these tasks. Ask parents to let you know if they have time to volunteer and which task(s) they wish to take responsibility for if they are able to assist. Next, schedule volunteer parents (working, where possible, within their time and space preferences). For example, typing can be done at home; the class newsletter can be published any day of the week; lunch count needs to be taken on Monday morning, but the book order is variable.

Parent volunteers can make more than just party plans—they can call chaperones for field trips and help solicit funds for class outings. Best of all, consider how you are tapping into the expertise of your parents and the community. Often volunteers would love to share their expertise in a particular area of interest with your class; they are just waiting for an invitation. (See Chapter 7 for more information on volunteers.)

The following is a letter I wrote to Room 6 parents at the beginning of our 1998-1999 school year.

new apartments in South Burlington. They are enjoying their new digs and are both getting used to life in this northern city. Jim's mom moved from Middlebury, Vermont, while my mom moved from Dedham, Massachusetts. I can't wait to see my mom's reaction to her first Vermont winter!

We will have a **Parents' Night** very early in the year. The date has been set for Wednesday, September 9, 1998, at 6:30 P.M. in Room 6. This will be a great evening for us to gather with ideas and questions about the year, and the "old fogey" parents will have lots of stories to share. This is a fun, informative evening, a wonderful chance to renew old friendships and begin new ones. Keep an eye out for more details shortly after school begins.

As you know, parent and community class volunteers are always welcome in Room 6! If you enjoy helping children in a particular curriculum area, working on activities such as the class newsletter, or reading with one or more students, this is the room for you! Please let me know if you have a particular and consistent time during the week that you could volunteer. We also welcome "drop-in" volunteers if your weekly schedule varies. Also, if you have a particular skill (e.g., sewing, building, music, etc.) you would like to share with us, please let me know. We look forward to seeing you in Room 6!

I have enclosed some information for you to peek at before school starts on Tuesday, September 1st. YIKES! I am getting so excited to see you all again, and I can't wait to meet and get to know all of our new parents, too!

I will be in school every day this week. If you would like to stop in and visit, please do! I still like to sleep late (some things will never change), so look for me in Room 6 after 10:00 a.m. On Monday, August 31st, I will be at school from 2:00 p.m. on until . . . who knows!

See you soon!

Sincerely, Ellen

Sample End-of-the-Summer Letter

Question & Answer

I want my first graders to have more classroom responsibilities. Will you suggest some appropriate jobs?

You would be surprised at how much a group of first graders can really help, and they will be eager and proud to take on every task. For example, students can

- take daily attendance, noting in the office folder who was absent
- check the weekly lunch-count tally, writing in the daily needs for the kitchen
- deliver information to the appropriate people and places
- collect snack drinks and pass them out
- keep track of reading time and update individual charts as needed
- place papers in mail cubbies or home-school folders
- feed classroom pets
- work on the newsletter writing committee
- edit newsletter stories
- serve as spelling and flash card buddies
- clean and set up the room
- organize and execute monthly fire drills; take fire drill attendance
- check and record the weather
- select and play quiet music during class workshop times

Think Outside the Box

Consider the many variables required of you in your teaching career. Now, start looking at some tasks differently. In other words, "think outside the box." It may appear to you that many of the day-to-day tasks on your list *have* to be completed in a similar fashion from year to year. Often, however, by chatting with other colleagues, attending a conference, or reading a new resource book, you will discover alternative, faster, and better ways to complete some of these tasks.

Bulletin Boards

Bulletin boards are not meant to be a source of competition, yet in many schools that is exactly what they are, with each teacher trying to outdo the next based on an arbitrary timeline devised years before. These bulletin boards often have nothing to do with the children and should therefore be eliminated from your list of tasks, giving back valuable time to you and your students.

Good bulletin boards should
- communicate and showcase new learning to others
- engage students in learning
- give students an audience to view their hard work
- create an interactive learning center

A Peek Inside Room 6

Student Bulletin Board

During our study of the rainforest one year I devised a culminating activity to showcase the students' work and share our knowledge with others through an exciting, informative, colorful, and creative display.

For this assignment the children worked in cooperative groups, which were formed by drawing names out of a hat. Each group was assigned a certain level of the rainforest—canopy, emergent, floor, and understory—and given a math problem to solve. Based on their written instructions, their task was to create a collage of different elements of their rainforest layer. They would show the results of their answer by cutting and pasting painted papers together. For instance, the group working on the canopy layer had to build four trees, each of a different height and width. No tree could be shorter than thirty-six inches, and no tree could be taller than sixty inches. In other words, they needed to come up with four trees of four different heights that could be no shorter than thirty-six inches and no taller than sixty inches. The group had to solve the problem first (i.e., decide on four different tree widths and heights), then create the trees.

As you can imagine, this was an intense project. I had several parent volunteers in the room to help with the initial reading of the problems. The students discussed what they were doing and why as they worked through the problems. Once the answer was in sight, they started to create the response piece for the mural. The adults in the room, me included, needed to give students their space at this point; we really wanted them to "own" the process. It may end up a little messier, but you can be sure that the end result will be one that students remember with pride!

The mural was gorgeous. Students used "community paper" (see page 58) we had painted ourselves (rather than regular construction paper). I had bought a roll of fadeless paper to use as the background. The "hot" green really livened things up. When it was complete, I posted each of the problems, along with the mural, on the wall.

Not only was the bulletin board an actual math problem-solving lesson, it also gave us a forum to showcase our rainforest knowledge for others.

Question & Answer

My principal expects me to change my bulletin boards often. How can I cut back on the time spent making and hanging these displays?

This is one area that can easily be completed in a teacher-friendly manner. I am sure that you and your class are constantly working on projects. These projects can become the material for your bulletin boards. Rather than trying to conjure up a new and cute display, try using students' actual theme-study work. These types of boards are much more reflective of your classroom instructional program and you are not constantly cutting out letters and manufactured pictures. I display our projects on the bulletin board, and then we turn it into a big book when work is taken down. Students are very proud of their work, and they love to see it on the big board!

What do you mean by "community paper"?

Community paper is a term coined by my art teacher/best friend, Ann Joppe-Mercure. She uses it to describe construction paper that has been painted over in order to add texture and depth. Our community paper projects are often created in the likeness of author/illustrator Eric Carle's work. We finger paint, bubble paint, sponge paint—you name it! The term "community" comes from the fact that once the paper is created, it belongs to the classroom community. (See Chapter 6 for various ways to decorate community paper.)

My school district wants teachers to keep track of and identify standards we address in our daily plans. That seems like a lot of work, and we're busy enough as it is. Is there an easy way to do this?

First, make sure you have your state's curriculum standards on your computer. They are actually easy to acquire, as most states include them on the Internet. You may try going directly to your state government's website, or you can try: www.achieve.org. This website is linked to all fifty state governor's offices and departments of education. Download standards from the Internet, and then take time to identify those standards applicable to a first-grade classroom. I usually look at standards for kindergarten and second-grade students, too, especially since my state chooses to group them K–4.

Now consider your class plans and create a form where the standards for each area can be printed below the time block. I plan my lessons for each time block and then I highlight the standards I plan to address during the lesson. This will take time initially, but your day-to-day time will be greatly reduced. Keep the empty form to photocopy and update with handwritten notes, or you can complete them right on your computer. With a marker, highlight the standards. Give a copy to your principal, and keep one for you!

Classroom Computer

A classroom computer can also help save time with certain tasks, especially those that might involve some repetition such as lesson plans and even substitute plans.

Lesson Plans and Weekly Schedule

Typing lesson plans on the computer allows greater flexibility in changing and re-vamping them as the week progresses. In the "olden" days, when everything was hand-written, teachers were less apt to update their plans. Now with plans on the computer, teachers can "cut and paste" to their heart's content! If your classroom instructional style makes much use of routines, place these in your files first. From now on you will only have to write/type in what is new and different for the class. (See page 47 for more information on weekly schedules.)

Substitute Plans

Enhance your substitute plans with the computer. At the beginning of each year, create a substitute folder that explains the major time blocks and routines used in your educational program. Keep plans in a three-ring binder along with the weekly schedule, and store the binder in the room. Also, reinforce the plans with a breakdown of class expectations for each day. Once you construct the basic format on the computer, use bits and pieces from one year to another to build a new set of substitute plans.

You can now spend more time describing the "flavor" of your classroom. And don't forget to share tips on how to interact with certain students. Also, describe in detail your teaching philosophy and class expectations. Your substitute will no doubt have his/her own teaching style, but make sure s/he understands your class and the guidelines you have created. (See Chapter 8 for more information on substitute plans.)

Class Newsletter

The class newsletter will improve greatly with the use of the computer. Its overall look and feel is one students will be proud to share and read with their families. You can use a special newsletter layout program, but the word processing program on your computer can be just as fun. (See Chapter 6 for more newsletter ideas.)

Overhead Projector

Use an overhead projector to help with whole-group instruction. Here you can make transparencies of student work or teacher-made worksheets. The projector saves on copying costs and clearly reproduces images and words on the wall. For example, I will often use the projector as an instructional tool for math lessons where I want the entire class to see the game board or form I am using.

Children may also use the overhead projector. In Room 6, this has become a favorite center during reading or writing workshop time. Make transparencies of favorite class poetry and/or songs, and let students project each piece on a wall. Now they can read and sing together while one student acts as "the teacher."

WIDELY HELD EXPECTATIONS FOR FIRST GRADERS: BENCHMARKS, STATE STANDARDS, AND ASSESSMENT TOOLS

Expectations. It is the first day of school. You are surrounded by twenty-seven six-year-olds, some smiling, some crying, others just plain bewildered. The room is buzzing with anxiety and excitement, and momentarily you panic as you suddenly see 179 more days stretch out in front of you. You wonder if your lesson plans and room arrangement will really work. You wonder what the classroom will feel and look like at the end of the school year. You wonder if you can fit the required state standards into your curriculum. You wonder what your students' and their parents' expectations are of first grade. And you hope your expectations will match theirs, knowing full-well you won't be able to satisfy everyone.

This chapter is designed to answer some of your most pressing questions—through Q&A's and reproducible tools—about benchmarks, standards, and assessments. With these aids in hand, you will be able to best position your students for learning.

Developmental Benchmarks

You won't be able to meet everyone's expectations, because people, including some parents, often have unrealistic goals for first graders. Perhaps the most profound misconception is that all first graders will learn to read during their first-grade year. And even more startling, they will all learn to read on the very first day of their first-grade year! And when the parents believe this, you can be sure the students believe it and are, therefore, both nervous and excited about starting this assignment.

Fortunately, there is a great deal of information on developmental benchmarks for all areas of children's growth—
- Social
- Emotional
- Physical
- Cognitive

If parents understand and accept these benchmarks, they will create a healthier, more realistic portrait of the year ahead. And by doing so, they will make your job and their child's school year a lot easier!

It is these benchmarks that let us educators know when to progress in certain areas and when to provide more time. And as all students are unique, these benchmarks also allow for us to best accommodate individual differences within the classroom.

Question & Answer

What do you mean by the term "benchmark"?

Benchmark refers to behavior that is characteristic of a child at different stages in his/her development. Teachers and parents need to consider the social, emotional, physical, and cognitive benchmarks of their students so they can create realistic expectations. Benchmarks also provide common ground on which teachers can measure their students' progress while keeping in mind that each student will progress to the prescribed level at his/her own pace.

Why is it that the children in my classroom display many different behaviors when they are all roughly the same age?

Growth and development are influenced by many factors, including culture, personality, and environment, and it is natural for children to work through developmental stages at different rates. That is why some of your first graders exhibit the behavior of a "typical" five-year-old, while others display the more mature behavior of a seven-year-old.

What about a child who is simply not ready for first grade—how can I convince his/her parents that their child would benefit from waiting a year?

This can be a difficult task as parents want naturally for their child to progress to the next level. Sometimes their reasons are conscientious—the child's younger sibling is advancing from kindergarten, and if the older child "stays back" they are afraid s/he will feel slighted. Unfortunately, some parents let their egos make the decision. In other words, it wouldn't "look good" for their child to repeat first grade; or, their child isn't "dumb," so why should s/he stay back? In a multiage program or a configuration in which children are not placed in traditional grades, the issue might not be as prevalent, but in a straight-grade situation, you need to show the parents concrete evidence that their child needs extra time. Portfolio work provides a representation of academic work, but how else might you convince them? Jim Grant's First-Grade Readiness Checklist (see adjacent page for sample) provides some helpful indicators for children's readiness, which you can share with parents.

Doing What Comes Naturally

Below are typical benchmarks most commonly associated with first graders.

Socially and emotionally, first graders
- love to be first
- are most concerned with themselves
- are competitive
- do not like to lose . . . anything!
- are loud, especially when upset
- do not always think before they respond

Physically, first graders
- grow and lose teeth
- can't sit still
- speak quickly
- move quickly
- try new things
- tire quickly

Cognitively, first graders
- want to learn everything at once
- are hands-on learners
- ask lots of questions
- learn cooperation
- play games
- form ideas
- discover new things every day

By making connections to known concepts, you are helping students learn and understand more and more information each day. You are setting the stage for lifelong learning.

Sample page from the First Grade Readiness Checklist, *by Jim Grant and Bob Johnson.*

Creating Your Classroom

How do you create a developmentally appropriate first-grade classroom with the best learning environment and curriculum? Below are some suggestions.

Environment
- Space to move around
- Quiet and cozy spaces

Time
- Time to take turns
- Opportunities to talk and be social
- Time to explore materials
- Rest time
- Less "line" time

Curriculum
- Short amounts of copy work
- Approximations in writing
- Curriculum studies connected to real experiences (e.g., field trips, hands-on learning)
- Curriculum standards incorporated into themes
- Cooperative academic situations

Activities
- Cooperative play situations
- Opportunities for dramatic play
- Opportunities to share materials
- Lots of new game experiences
- Less competitive activities
- Artistic opportunities (e.g., art, drama, music)
- Large-motor/fine-motor activities

General
- Support and encouragement to slow down
- Opportunities to do for themselves

Question & Answer

Why does the brightest child in my classroom throw temper tantrums when things do not go his way?

A child's social and cognitive development do not always grow at the same rate. The same child reading Macbeth in my classroom during silent reading would throw a fit when his shoe came untied! All children, even your brightest students, need time and practice in order to move forward in their development.

Remember that benchmarks are important indicators of typical behaviors at specific ages, but they may vary—sometimes slightly, sometimes dramatically—for each student.

Standards

Today, the call for tougher curriculum standards is being broadcast throughout the United States. And as each state has its own strict standards-based assessment system, it is no wonder that educators are more than a little confused and frustrated as to how to balance instruction and curriculum add-ons with what we know—developmentally, cognitively, socially, and emotionally—about this age group.

Russian psychologist Lev Vygotsky believed that children learn first through social interaction and second through internal reasoning. He also believed that teaching children within close range of their current ability would yield more positive results than teaching at their frustration level. This "zone of proximal development," as Vygotsky labeled it, should make sense to most teachers and parents, but when faced with an ever-increasing curriculum load, a prolific standards movement, extracurricular instruction, and lack of time, it becomes difficult to treat each student as the unique individual s/he is. This is why it is so important for teachers to incorporate age-level information with academic benchmark pieces in order to assess what should be through whole-group instruction, small-group instruction, or one-on-one conferencing.

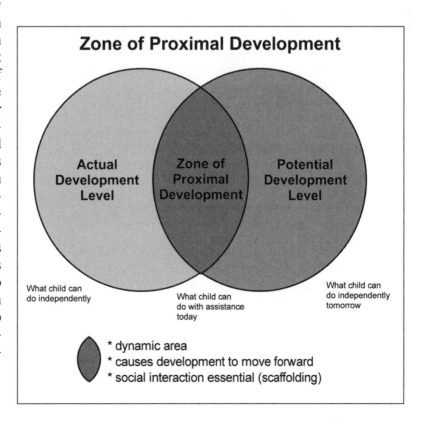

Zone of Proximal Development

Actual Development Level — What child can do independently

Zone of Proximal Development — What child can do with assistance today

Potential Development Level — What child can do independently tomorrow

* dynamic area
* causes development to move forward
* social interaction essential (scaffolding)

First Steps: Incorporating Standards into Your Curriculum
You can better get to know and understand your students through
- observation
- student profile sheets (to be filled out by students during the summer)
- checklists and surveys
- assessments and evaluations
- summer conferences with parents

When applied in the classroom, these approaches can help meet individual needs while also meeting standards; parents will appreciate your efforts in getting to know them and their children; and you will be able to start creating goals for the entire class and individual students.

Once you have gained this information, you should consider the curriculum you are expected to teach and your students are expected to learn. Start by reading your state's grade-level standards. Some districts break the standards down for the district-wide curriculum, but you can find published standards at your state department of education (on line and on paper), at your central office, and through published books on national standards. If you don't know the web address of your state's education department, try: www.achieve.org. This website contains links to all fifty departments of education.

In Vermont, the standards are set into by developmental chunks like this:

Reading Strategies

1.1 Students use a variety of strategies to help them read. This is evident when students use a combination of strategies including: PreK–4
   a. Sounds, syllables, and letter patterns (e.g., phonological, phonic, and graphic knowledge);
   b. Syntax;
   c. Meaning in context;
   d. A range of cuing systems to discover pronunciation and meaning;
   e. Self-correcting when subsequent reading indicates an earlier miscue;
   f. Questioning; and
   g. Prior knowledge of the topic and sense of story.

1.2 Students read grade-appropriate material, with 90%+ accuracy, in a way that makes meaning clear.

Reading Comprehension

1.3 Students read for meaning, demonstrating both initial understanding and personal response to what is read. This is evident when students: PreK–4
   a. Comprehend grade-appropriate materials;
   b. Analyze and interpret features of a variety of types of text; and
   c. Make connections among various parts of a text, among several texts, and between texts and other experiences in and out of school.

Here is an actual sample from Vermont's standards.

Your classroom is a microcosm of the world, and as such, some students will meet and surpass standards while others will inevitably struggle. Children experiencing difficulties should be referred to *Reading Recovery*, Title I, Special Education, or another early-literacy intervention program, as all students deserve the support and good teaching it takes to do the best they can.

And remember: don't let standards loom over your room like a dark cloud. Standards are none other than those concepts you introduce into your curriculum. In the following chapters I provide some fun and creative ideas on how to incorporate standards into your daily lessons. Be prepared and organized, but have fun with your students along the way.

Assessment Tools

Assessment is a vital component of your instructional decision-making, but it does not have to be as scary or as time-consuming as you might imagine. Keep in mind that without assessment, you are determining each student's academic status based on assumptions. With assessment, however, you have in hand concrete evidence for each student with which you are able to positively impact his/her educational needs through properly determined instruction.

How do you define assessment? Evaluation?

Assessment:
  the information we gather.

Evaluation:
  what we do with the information.

Teaching is the use of this specific child-centered information to support the student in moving to the next step of his/her own learning.

My school year calendar is divided into quarters, and therefore I fill out a district report card four times a year.

Report cards are accompanied by a narrative profile about each child and an overview of everything—curricular and otherwise—that has been happening in Room 6. I was able to construct these evaluation pieces from various assess-ments conducted the previous quarter(s). Assessment is a continuous and integral part of everything I do. Without it, I would be unable to fine-tune my lesson plans, and individual goal-setting—a direct product of assessment

and such a vital part of each student's success—would be haphazard guesswork.

When looking at assessment pieces, ask these three questions:
1. What does the student know?
2. What does the student need to know?
3. What do I, as a teacher, need to do to help the student learn?

Formative and Summative Assessments

Formative assessments: assessments you give frequently—a reading survey, spelling questionnaire, or student conference sheet. Formative assessments help you decide, for example, which learning structure (e.g., flexible grouping, one-on-one work, pair work) is best for each student.

Summative assessments: a grade on a project or report card—"sums up" what students know at the end of a unit or term. You need summative assessments for record-keeping and for informing parents and possibly specialists of each student's overall progress in the learning continuum.

It is important to remind parents that all students are on that learning continuum, but they are not all at the same point. It is your responsibility to determine where each child is located and teach him/her from that point. Be a child-driven teacher, however, *not* a content-driven teacher. In our standards-based society, it is sometimes difficult not to fall into the role of the latter.

Formative Assessment Made Easy

Consider what information you will need to gather during the year. How you choose to do this is the crux of the assessment dilemma. I suggest you

- use multiple assessments
- gather work samples frequently
- imbed assessment into your daily instructional program

By following this advice, you will gather important, on-the-spot information and save valuable time during report card season.

Question & Answer

Are there any good resource books that would help me develop the tools to accurately assess my students?

Yes! There are many books that share good examples of "authentic" assessment tools. These tools are meant to become part of your instructional program. My favorite books on assessment are: *The Whole Language Catalog: Forms for Authentic Assessment*, by Lois Bird, and *Classroom Based Assessment*, by Bonnie Campbell Hill, Cynthia Ruptic, and Lisa Norwick. Both of these resources share real assessment tools that, with little revision, you can use in your own classroom. The second book even comes with the forms on CD—what a time-saver!

Record-Keeping

Imbed assessment pieces into your instructional practices. You will find that administering these assessments will become second nature and not just another add-on. In order to best do this, however, devise an easy-to-use record-keeping system so that you can instantly retrieve and store information. Remember: keep your system manageable. When it becomes over-whelming, I, for one, tend to revert to systems that are less efficient.

Here's what I suggest: Use large three-ring binders to store information and work samples—in separate folders—for each student. (I call this my teacher portfolio. You will find that, depending on the size of your class, you will need more than one binder.) Inside each student folder, include student work samples and formal assessments from each curriculum area. For language arts assessments, for example, I include among others, a

- literacy assessment (see page 81 for more information)
- spelling survey (see page 81 for more information)
- reading inventory (see pages 81-82)
- peer conference sheet (see page 83)

(For a complete listing, see the 9-week Assessment Cycle on page 75.)

These assessments pinpoint students' strengths and weaknesses, and they help you focus on what kind of information you gather and how you gather it. You will find these assessment tools are especially helpful when conferencing with parents and school specialists.

When and How Assessment Takes Place

Assessment with children takes place through formal and informal methods, including

- interaction
- observation
- analysis

Assessment is a "child-heavy" component. In other words, you need the children present in order for two out of three of these techniques to work. Thus, it is critical you reserve time in your daily/weekly schedule in order to best interact with and observe students. It is also important that you invent easy record-keeping methods—informative yet convenient ways in which to gather information on each of your students.

Interaction with Students: Conferences

Use simple conference recording sheets (see pages 72-74 for book, writing, and math conference tally recording sheet reproducibles) for your academic time blocks. Conference sheets will become part of your teacher portfolio binder and will remind you to ask different, questions such as the instructional level of a book, a math activity, or a writing piece. They will also give you a place to keep track of the titles and activities your students choose.

When meeting with students for reading instruction, I recommend you take a running record for every book they read. This record gives you instant information about the text-level appropriateness for the student and how the student is currently manipulating text. (See page 80 for more information on running records.)

Book Conference Tally

Student Name: Gregory   Date: 11/2/98

Date	Book Read	Project Paper	Type of Book	Running Record
9/4	The Meanies	Main idea	Just right	✔
9/6	Dan, the Flying Man	Setting	Just right	
9/7	Brown Bear, Brown Bear	Favorite part	Easy	
9/10	Just Go to Bed	Characters	Just right /hard	✔
9/12	The Very Hungry Caterpillar	Setting	Just right	

1. **Book Read**: List title of book being shared.
2. **Project Paper**: Record which project paper the student chose and completed. Encourage student to try them all. Each one centers on a different skill.
3. **Type of Book**: Ask the child: "Is the book 'just right' (a good instructional level book)?" Why? Why not? Use the terms: *just right*, *hard*, or *easy* to classify books.
4. **Running Record**: Place a ✓ in this column if a running record has been done at the conference.

Writing Conference Tally

Student Name: Nathaniel   Date: 10/1/98

Date	Story/Piece	I Am Working on...	I Can Do...
9/20	My Cat	Using periods at the ends of my sentences.	Label pictures. Describe the pictures.
9/27	Dogs I Like	Using capital letters at the beginning of my sentences.	use capital letters on names.

1. **Story/piece**: List title of writing being shared.
2. **I Do**: Record your conference conversation in regard to what the child is demonstrating in his/her writing. These will reflect the use of organization, details, purpose, voice, and/or grammar usage and mechanics skills.
3. **I Am Working on:** Discuss with the child his/her next step. From the writing, choose a skill the student is beginning to understand. Instruct him/her further on the use of this skill. Ask the student to edit the piece, paying particular attention to the skill you just discussed.

Math Conference Tally

Student Name: Michelle   Date: 3/10/98

Date	Currently Working on . . .	I Can Do . . .	I Need to Work on . . .	Papers
9/10	Computation facts to 10	Addition to 10 manipulatives	Numeral formation	✔
9/15	Basic geometric shapes	Square, rectangle, circle, triangle	Oval trapezoid	✔
	Estimation of less than 25 objects	Counting to 100		
9/22	Using pattern blocks to reproduce and create pictures	Trapezoid	Spatial relationships	

1. **Currently Working on**: Record the math skill being taught at this time.
2. **I Can Do**: Record newly acquired skills in math, based on activity choice, observations, paperwork, and conversation with the student.
3. **I Need to Work on**: Discuss next steps with the student. Instruct with new learning in mind.
4. **Papers**: Place a ✔ in this column if math papers have been given at the conference.

While assessment may seem overwhelming, it won't be if you:

- Schedule time during the day to observe children
- Schedule time in your instructional program where you meet one-on-one with children
- Keep the number of assessment pieces manageable
- Keep the number of times you assess manageable
- Take time to reflect on the information you have gathered
- Begin the summative process early. Do not postpone until the night before a parent conference
- Assess those areas that will affect your teaching decisions
- Assess to answer your questions about a student
- Are in control of the assessment and use it to inform your instructional practices. (See page 65 for information on the Zone of Proximal Development.)

Book Conference Tally

Student Name: _____   Date: _____

Date	Book Read	Project Paper	Type of Book	Running Record

1. **Book Read**: List title of book being shared.
2. **Project Paper**: Record which project paper the child chose and completed. Encourage child to try them all. Each one centers on a different skill.
3. **Type of Book**: Ask the child: "Is the book 'just right' (a good instructional level book)?" Why? Why not? Use the terms: *just right*, *hard*, or *easy* to classify books.
4. **Running Record**: Place a ✔ in this column if a running record has been done at the conference.

Reproducible

Writing Conference Tally

Student Name: _____   Date: _____

Date	Story/Piece	I Am Working on . . .	I Can Do . . .

1. **Story/Piece**: List title of writing being shared.
2. **I Am Working on:** Discuss with the child his/her next step. From the writing, choose a skill the student is beginning to understand. Instruct him/her further on the use of this skill. Ask the student to edit the piece, paying particular attention to the skill you just discussed.
3. **I Can Do**: Record your conference conversation in regard to what the child is demonstrating in his/her writing. These will reflect the use of organization, details, purpose, voice, and/or grammar usage and mechanics skills.

Reproducible

Math Conference Tally

Student Name: _____   Date: _____

Date	Currently Working on . . .	I Can Do . . .	I Need to Work on . . .	Papers

1. **Currently Working on**: Record the math skill being taught at this time.
2. **I Can Do**: Record newly acquired skills in math based on activity choice, observations, paperwork, and conversation with the student.
3. **I Need to Work on**: Discuss next steps with the student. Instruct with new learning in mind.
4. **Papers**: Place a ✔ in this column if math papers have been given at the conference.

Language Arts Assessment Tools:
When to Administer Assessments

The 9-Week Assessment Cycle below shows the balance in my literacy assessments and it provides me with a clear visual of Room 6 curriculum instruction and assessment procedures. Use this cycle to determine approximate times for administering assessments during each marking period.

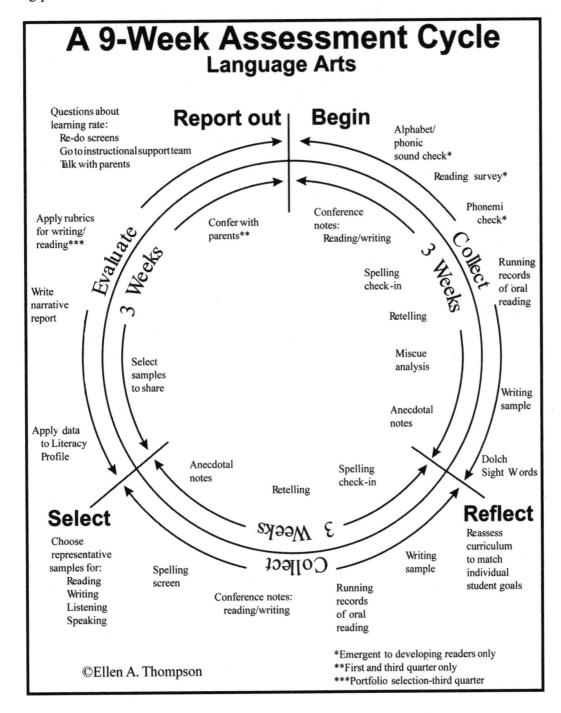

A 9-Week Assessment Cycle
Language Arts

Questions about learning rate:
Re-do screens
Go to instructional support team
Talk with parents

Report out | **Begin**

Alphabet/ phonic sound check*

Reading survey*

Phonemi check*

Apply rubrics for writing/ reading***

Confer with parents**

Conference notes: Reading/writing

Evaluate

3 Weeks

Collect

3 Weeks

Spelling check-in

Running records of oral reading

Retelling

Write narrative report

Miscue analysis

Select samples to share

Writing sample

Anecdotal notes

Apply data to Literacy Profile

Anecdotal notes

Spelling check-in

Dolch Sight Words

Retelling

3 Weeks

Collect

Select

Reflect

Choose representative samples for:
Reading
Writing
Listening
Speaking

Spelling screen

Conference notes: reading/writing

Running records of oral reading

Writing sample

Reassess curriculum to match individual student goals

©Ellen A. Thompson

*Emergent to developing readers only
**First and third quarter only
***Portfolio selection-third quarter

Language Arts 9-Week Assessment Cycle Explanations

1. Alphabet/Phonics Sound Check: Do this basic assessment one-on-one with students. In random order, show each child the letters of the alphabet—uppercase and lowercase. Ask them to name the letter and say a word in which this letter sound is represented. Record the response and store in your teaching portfolio.

2. Reading Survey: This is a set of questions about reading attitudes. Record the answers. I suggest you perform this assessment at the beginning of the year and again at the end of the year. (See page 81 for more information on the Burke Reading Inventory; see page 82 for Reading Inventory reproducible.)

3. Phonemic Check: This is a quick check for assessing each student's ability to hear phonemes within words. Use a list of words. Say the words out loud. The student responds (using blocks, chips, etc.) with how many parts s/he can hear in the word.

4. Running Records of Oral Reading: While listening to a student read, use a notation system to record exactly what s/he is saying. Assess students' comprehension and use of the three cueing systems. (See page 80 for more information on running records; see page 80 for more information on the three cueing systems.)

5. Writing Sample: Collect a representative writing sample from the student's independent writing. You will most likely find good samples in the student's conversation journal or process-writing folder in which *all* drafts of the story (sloppy copy and all) should be stored.

6. Dolch Sight Words: Check each student for sight-word knowledge against a list of the 220 most commonly used words. (See page 77 for word list.)

7. Conference Notes for Reading and Writing: Keep notes on each individual student. Note
   - books students are reading/stories they are writing
   - instructional level of their work
   - comprehension
   - grammar
   - spelling

8. Spelling: Students work with lists of words—a combination of words from their own writing and the sight-word list, which is part of the word wall vocabulary.

9. Retelling: Meet with each student and ask him/her to "retell" a story. Listen for
   - fluency
   - details
   - sequence of events

10. Miscue Analysis: This assessment is similar to a running record. The difference is that the record of oral reading is done from a pre-published "graded" reading passage. Perform a miscue analysis at least three times a year with your young readers. Miscue packages can be bought from almost any book publisher, but first check with your district Title I program to see which forms they use.

11. Anecdotal Notes: Anecdotal notes document the real classroom stories of each student's learning growth—real stories with real names. Anecdotals personalize your parent conferences, as you are able to share a child's academic journey. Perhaps most importantly, anecdotal notes chart each student's progress in a way that pencil/paper tests do not. (See page 69 for more information on record-keeping.)

Dolch Sight Words

PREPRIMER	PRIMER		FIRST	SECOND	THIRD
a	all	went	after	always	about
and	am	what	again	around	better
away	are	white	an	because	bring
big	at	who	any	been	carry
blue	ate	will	as	before	clean
can	be	with	ask	best	cut
come	black	yes	by	both	done
down	brown		could	buy	draw
find	but		every	call	drink
for	came		fly	cold	eight
funny	did		from	does	fall
go	do		give	don't	far
help	eat		going	fast	full
hers	four		had	first	got
I	get		has	five	grow
in	good		her	found	hold
is	has		him	gave	hot
it	he		how	goes	hurt
jump	into		just	green	if
little	like		know	its	keep
look	must		let	made	kind
make	new		live	many	laugh
me	no		may	off	light
my	now		of	or	long
not	on		old	pull	much
one	our		once	read	myself
play	out		open	right	never
red	please		over	sing	only
run	pretty		put	sit	own
said	ran		round	sleep	pick
see	ride		some	tell	seven
the	saw		stop	their	shall
three	say		take	these	show
to	she		thank	those	six
two	so		them	upon	small
up	soon		then	us	start
we	that		think	use	ten
yellow	there		walk	very	today
you	they		where	wash	try
	this		when	which	warm
	too			why	
	under			wish	
	want			work	
	was			would	
	well			write	
				yours	

Evaluation: Language Arts 9-Week Assessment Cycle

1. Apply data to each student's literacy profile. For example, by this time I should have answered the following questions about each student's literacy profile:

   - How familiar is the student with print and the world of books?

   - To what extent is the student learning the strategies/processes associated with reading?

   - Is the student able to read books of increasing complexity?

   - How is the student's oral language developing?

   - Is the student developing investigative, research, and presentation skills?

   - How well does the student understand and respond to what is read?

   - How is the student's independent writing developing with regard to purpose, organization, details, and voice/tone?

   - Is the student developing effective writing processes and strategies?

   - Is the student developing an ability to reflect on his/her reading and writing, and revise/adjust accordingly?

   - How engaged is the student when reading and writing?

   For my literacy profile I use the *Primary Literacy/Communication Profile*, developed in 1996 for Vermont teachers by Sue Biggam, Nancy Herman, and Shayne Trubisz. This profile provides descriptive language for language arts development for grades K–4.

   Analyze your collection against the language of the profiles you use and determine at what level each student is currently working.

2. Read through your student portfolios and select student samples to share with parents at conferences.

3. Apply rubrics to writing/reading samples. Take a representative writing/reading sample from each student and apply each to the rubrics used in your school district. (See pages 86-89 for more information on rubrics.)

4. Write a narrative report (see page 79) for each student by reviewing and combining information on school work, literacy profile, math profile, and rubrics. The rubrics and profiles will help provide the parents with concrete evidence of where the student stands academically. The anecdotal records will give your report a more personal feel. End your narrative with the "next steps" a student should take. And discuss with parents what they should see in their child's academic development and how they can support their child in his/her learning.

Here's an example of a parent letter.

First Quarter Report: Richard*

November 15, 1998

Richard's latest reading miscue shows him to be manipulating print comfortably at a beginning first-grade level. When given this miscue in September, Richard did not feel comfortable enough to "read" it as a story, but instead told me the words he knew (is, the, a, Sam). By October he felt more secure and attempted the piece as a story, that is, he read it from left to right and from top to bottom. While he still missed many words, his willingness to try it was admirable. As you know, Richard takes this learning-to-read business very seriously! He is extremely honest about his attempts and he will not give himself credit for partial learning—it is all or nothing.

Richard's writing is coming along very well. He expresses his thoughts in sequence, and his spelling patterns fall into a semi-phonetic spelling level, which is quite good given his age. That means that much of his writing is still driven by phonics and particularly the phonetic sounds of consonants. In addition, Richard is not sure of his vowel sounds in his writing. He does contribute to our class lessons about vowels, so I do know he is getting the hang of all of this. His writing skills have increased dramatically since the first day of school, as you know. He works hard at it and it really shows.

Richard has done well on his spelling words. He has had three spelling check-ins and has learned nine out of fourteen words given. These spelling words are taken directly from his own story writing. These are words he uses frequently and therefore should be spelled correctly as time goes on.

Math is fun for Richard. He loves playing strategy games such as Mancala, Senet, and Abalone. He does well with his addition practice, and he will be beginning subtraction work within the week. Richard needs to work on learning his basic addition and subtraction facts up to ten. He becomes anxious when he has to make a choice for himself at math time (and Free-Choice Time), and he tends to wait for someone to choose for him.

Richard, however, does very well with his homework assignments. He has remembered and completed his homework four out of five times.

Richard is getting more comfortable in the classroom. He has friends he "hangs" out with, and at the end of the day he will talk with me about all of the things he is involved with both at home and at school. I do worry about his anxiety at times, however; he really struggles to perform tasks that are meant to be fun, not scary! On the other hand, he is taking more risks, and I find him much more independent now than at the beginning of the year. He is a very capable student, but he waits for affirmation for everything he does. Somehow, Richard needs to value his decisions himself. This is no easy task, I realize. When I assign him a job, I literally have to turn around so he can complete it himself. He does, although sometimes he really tries to wait me out.

Be proud of your son's accomplishments and assist him on feeling good about his work.

I look forward to meeting with you in the near future.

Sincerely,

Ms. T

* Student's actual name was not used in this report.

More on Language Arts Assessments

The running record and Burke Reading Inventory are explained in greater depth below. In addition, I have provided information on the spelling survey, the Peer Conference Sheet, and the Think Aloud. These assessment tools allow you to pinpoint where your students are on the learning continuum.

Running Record

With beginning readers especially, it is important to stay up-to-date with their ever-evolving reading abilities. Running records will help you capture this reading development in print.

A running record is just that, a record of the child's reading. My students always read to me during a book conference, and with pencil and paper in hand, I record their reading with shorthand symbols first made popular by the *Reading Recovery* program. Once the reading is recorded, I analyze it. I want to know, for example, if the reader is making use of the three cueing systems and if s/he favors one more than the others. This information informs what instructional steps I will take next with that child.

Question & Answer

What are the three cueing systems that a reader needs to use?

A reader needs to use the following cueing systems:
- Semantic—contextual cues
- Syntactic—grammatical cues
- Graphophonic—phonics cues

Do you know of any good books that discuss running records in depth?

Yes, I recommend two books:

 The Early Detection of Reading Difficulties, by Marie Clay

Running Records; A Self-Tutoring Guide (audio tape), by Peter Johnston

Spelling Survey

Spelling, as you know, is a BIG word in first-grade classrooms. Parents and children should understand just how important it is, but they should also keep in mind what we know about how young children learn to spell—through seeing print and writing as important communication tools. In other words, extend parents' and students' definition of spelling instruction: spelling is not simply a means by which to memorize words for a test.

The spelling survey in ▯ *Teaching Spelling: A Practical Resource,* by Faye Bolton and Diane Snowball, is an informative tool I use to gather information from parents at the beginning of the year. This survey is nonthreatening and it highlights spelling instruction issues and provides a basis for your conversation with parents. Parents fill out this form, but teachers can also use it to consider their own practices—a great faculty meeting discussion topic.

Reading Inventory

I love to chat with students at the beginning of the year and throughout the year about the reading process. The Burke Reading Inventory (see page 82) is a wonderful, nonthreatening assessment tool that helps uncover children's attitudes toward reading and is a real eye-opener for many parents! I share these student conversations with their parents at the first conference.

To create your own reading survey:
- Brainstorm ten or more questions to ask your students at the start and at the end of the school year
- Record answers during informal conversations
- Share responses with parents at the first and last conferences of the year

This survey will give you a forum in which to discuss the fact that children are more likely to become lifelong readers if they witness reading at home.

> ### Burke Reading Inventory
>
> 1. What books do you like best? Why?
> Barney, Jurassic Park. I like dinosaurs. They're cute if they have fur like Barney.
>
> 2. Do you read and/or listen to stories at home?
> I have a few taped stories I get from the library. Mom reads at night sometimes.
>
> 3. Who reads to you at home? Mom.
>
> 4. Who do you see that reads and what do they read?
> My brother reads sometimes, lots of stuff, Berenstein Bears. Mom—books, any kind. She's working on a few right now.
>
> 5. Why do people read?
> It's good for your brain. It tells you stuff that you never knew was in books. They do it just 'cause they like to.
>
> 6. What do you already know about how to read?
> Comics in the newspaper—but it has to be a BIG word so I can see it.
>
> 7. What else would you like to read better?
> I would like to read a whole book. I get really tired sounding out words.
>
> 8. When you are reading and you come to a word you do not know, what do you do?
> Look around for it somewhere. Sound it out. Close the book and stop (take a rest).
>
> 9. Who do you think is a good reader? Mom.
>
> 10. What does that person do that makes him/her a good reader?
> She's been reading a lot. That's true; she reads a lot!
>
> 11. Tell me what goes on in your head when you read.
> If it doesn't have pictures, you make them up. Make the picture in your head.
>
> L. Bird, et al. *The Whole Language Catalog.* New York: McGraw-Hill, 1997. Reprinted with permission from The McGraw-Hill Companies.

Sample Burke Reading Inventory

You might also consider purchasing ▯ *Developmental Reading Assessment,* by Joetta Beaver. This comprehensive resource helps K–3 teachers monitor reading behaviors and conduct periodic assessments within their literature-based reading program.

Burke Reading Inventory

1. What books do you like best? Why?

2. Do you read and/or listen to stories at home?

3. Who reads to you at home?

4. Who do you see that reads and what do they read?

5. Why do people read?

6. What do you already know about how to read?

7. What else would you like to read better?

8. When you are reading and you come to a word you do not know, what do you do?

9. Who do you think is a good reader?

10. What does that person do that makes him/her a good reader?

11. Tell me what goes on in your head when you read.

L. Bird, et al. The Whole Language Catalog. *New York: McGraw-Hill, 1997. Reprinted with permission from The McGraw-Hill Companies.*

Reproducible

Peer Conference Sheet

Review the Peer Conference Sheet with students (see below) and discuss all terms. In order to complete this form, students first need to finish a writing piece, one they would like to publish for an audience. Next, students should hold a conference with one of their peers and use the conference sheet to prompt discussion about their writing. The form and this conference really start students thinking about the attributes of quality writing. While the questions may seem difficult, with proper instruction, students will hold excellent conferences with one another.

Teach the terms on the conference sheet—using a well-written children's story, for example—through whole-group mini-lessons at the very beginning of writing workshop time. You will most likely find that at this age, students' conversations are stronger than what they actually write down on paper, as their fine-motor abilities are still developing.

Room 6 students complete a peer conference sheet for each book they write. Sometimes they work on this form with an adult volunteer or an instructional support person. After they have written three books, they decide which book they would like to publish.

Peer Conference Sheet

Student Name: _____ Title of your story:_____

Peer Name: _____

Purpose: Is the purpose of the story clear? Will my audience understand what I am trying to write about?
_____

Organization: Does my story make sense from beginning to end? Have I repeated things in my story?
_____

Details: Have I added details to my story? Will it "paint" pictures in the minds of my audience?
_____

Voice/Tone: Have I put "me" on the paper? Can I tell that "I" wrote it?
_____

Grammar/usage/mechanics: Did I check for capital letters in the right places? Did I put in periods, question marks, or exclamation marks? Did I circle words that I need help with for spelling?
_____

Do you have any suggestions for my story?
_____

What was your favorite part of my story? Why?
_____

The questions on this sheet follow the language from the original Vermont Writing Rubric, *used as part of our state-wide assessment. I have taken the five attributes of quality writing and have put the language into question form for students to use during their conference. As always, I review and discuss this form and conferencing time with them before they work on it independently.*

Contact your state department of education for such forms, and try using the form's language with children so they will be comfortable with the process before similar assessments are administered in later grades.

Think Aloud

As students become more proficient readers, some may start to choose longer stories to read. A running record may not give you enough information about the story and the students' comprehension of the story, but a Think Aloud form (see page 85) will. A Think Aloud is simple to use. It allows you the opportunity to listen to and record what a student is doing while s/he reads. Here's what you do:

- Ask one student to share what s/he is currently reading
- Ask the questions on the form
- Scribe the answers
- Student goes back to reading silently

After the conference, take time to analyze what the student's comments indicate about his/her reading of the story. Important questions to ask include:

- Is s/he reading for meaning?
- Was s/he able to recall important information?
- Could the student articulate reading strategies s/he used (e.g., looking at pictures, sounding out words, rereading)?
- Is the text level appropriate for the reader?

Add the Think Aloud form to each student's folder in your teacher portfolio.

Spelling Screen

A spelling screen allows you to peek in and "see" what students are doing when it comes to their own independent spelling. Spelling-screen words are not words students study. Rather, the words on this screen incorporate and represent a myriad of spelling skills that a first grader should learn in your classroom. The screen indicates which skills the student has, in fact, inculcated into his/her learning.

I suggest you share students' screens with their parents at conference time. Generate a list with parents called "What does your child know right now when it comes to spelling these words?" At your final parent conference of the year, share a spelling screen from the beginning of the year and from the end of the year. This really allows parents to "see" their child's growth. This screen, coupled with the spelling questionnaire, should help parents understand what you mean when you discuss instructional practices and children's developmental levels in spelling. In addition, a spelling screen moves your conversation into a discussion of good spelling as a communication tool, versus spelling just to score well on a test.

Question & Answer

Where might I find information on spelling screens?

I recommend three books:
- *Understanding Reading Problems: Assessment and Instruction,* by Jean Wallace Gillet
- *Spelling for Whole Language Classrooms,* by Ethel Buchanan
- *Teaching Kids to Spell: A Workshop Approach,* by Richard Gentry

Think Aloud

Student Name: _____ Date: _____

Text: _____

Big Idea	Strategies
What was important in the part you just read?	What were you doing as you read that part? Strategies?
Teacher Comments:	

Prompts

Narrative Text
- Who else is in the story?
- When/where did that happen?
- What else happened? Can you tell me more about that part?
- What was the problem? How was it solved?
- What do you think will be in the next part?

Expository Text
- What was the main thing the author wanted you to learn?
- What other important information did the author tell?
- What other facts do you remember?
- Do you have any questions about this story?

Reproducible

Analysis
Rubrics

Share rubric criteria with students before the activity—not after—so they know what they need to do in order to successfully understand and complete a task.

Create Your Own Rubric

Create your own rubric for any curriculum area by following the instructions below.

1. Decide what criteria is applicable to this particular curriculum assessment piece. (Consult with your district/state standards.)
2. List and describe rubric criteria by using the lables below.
   - Above and Beyond (1)
   - Right on Target (2) *Note: this is considered at benchmark*
   - Almost There (3)
   - Just Beginning (4)

Curriculum Area: _____

Criteria for: How familiar is the student with print and the world of books.

Above and Beyond (1):

Has most concepts of print, including functions of simple punctuation. Student demonstrates consistent control over concepts of print in reading.

Right on Target (2):

Has control over voice-print matching. Understands differences between upper and lowercase print.

Almost There (3):

Has control over left-right directionality and return sweep. May not have voice-print matching. Understands differences between upper and lowercase print.

Just Beginning (4):

Has some concepts of print. Can recognize own name. Does not pay much attention to print.

Reproducible

I Teach First Grade 91

Question & Answer

I hear the word "rubric" all the time. What does it mean?

A rubric is an assessment tool that helps teachers measure students' work against a particular standard/criterion or set of standards/criteria. You can consult with your district office for curriculum standards, as pre-made rubric sheets may already be available, or you can develop your own curriculum rubrics (see page 87) to assess a process, activity, task, or product. A third option is to purchase a book of reproducible rubrics from an educational publishing group.

Create Your Own Rubric

Create your own rubric for any curriculum area by following the instructions below.

1. Decide what criteria is applicable to this particular curriculum assessment piece. (Consult with your district/state standards.)
2. List and describe rubric criteria by using the lables below.
    - Above and Beyond (1)
    - Right on Target (2) *Note: this is considered at benchmark*
    - Almost There (3)
    - Just Beginning (4)

Curriculum Area: _____
Criteria for: _____
Above and Beyond (I):
Right on Target (2):
Almost There (3):
Just Beginning (4):

Use a rubric to chart the oral retelling of a book a student has just read (see page 89). Scribe the retelling or tape it. Then, using a rubric, analyze the retelling. Taping the student gives you the opportunity to listen to the selection a second time—without interruption. The one dilemma with taping is the amount of background noise recorders pick up. If you do decide to tape, try to find a quiet area.

Curriculum Area: Language Arts

Criteria for: Retelling a Story

Above and Beyond (1): Student uses own voice to show author's craft. Retells with fluency. Gives information about characters and setting, adding own sight and background knowledge. Uses story structure appropriately. Does not dwell on unnecessary information.

Right on Target (2): Retells the story, giving attention to key story parts. Independently identifies major plot elements, story characters, and setting. Uses story structure in his/her oral language.

Almost There (3): Gives basic information about story. Includes unnecessary information as well. May need some prompting. Tends to confuse the sequence of events.

Just Beginning (4): The retelling shows confusion about the order of the story. Key elements are missing. Can respond to questions about characters and setting. Prompting is needed.

Criteria for Retelling a Story (Anecdotal Note Form)

Student Name: _____ Date: _____

Describe the quality of the student's retelling in the following areas:

Fluency:

Awareness of author's craft:

Voice:

Describe if the student was able to recall and describe each of the following:

Characters:

Setting:

Plot retelling:

Use of story structure language (e.g., beginning, next, then, character, setting, plot, problem, climax, resolution, personal reaction):

Observation

The most important information we gather are the actual conversations—the pictures, if you will—of children working together. These stories constitute the bulk of what is commonly referred to as anecdotal records, snippets of day-to-day life. They should be positive pictures that tell you something about each student's progress. Though it is sometimes difficult to find the time, take a few minutes to jot down these stories, making sure to complete one or more for each of your students.

The Easy Anecdotal Record

I recommend using sticky labels for your anecdotal notes.

Here's what to do:

- Buy sticky labels for computer printing at office supply stores or through supply catalogs.
- At the beginning of the year, print out a class set with each student's name across the top.
- Place this sheet on a clipboard and begin your anecdotal notes.
- Fill one entire sticky label sheet before moving on to the next sheet.
- When all the sticky labels on one sheet have been filled with notes, file them in each student's folder, located in your teacher's portfolio binder. (Set aside several blank pages in the students' folders on which to place the sticky labels.)

Make sure you gather anecdotal notes on each of your students. You now have great, informative information at your fingertips for report card time!

Self-Evaluation

- Teachers need to do this
- Kids need to do this

Self-evaluation and student evaluation are healthy, eye-opening practices. It is important to check and evaluate what you *think* is being learned in your classroom. After twenty-two years of teaching, I have learned never to assume anything! I have also learned that if my students are not "getting" something, the reason usually has more to do with me that it does with them. It is at these times I need to evaluate what and how I am teaching; I need to determine the best instructional match for my students and reconsider the material we are learning.

Writing As Part of Reflection

Journals and free-write situations allow students and teachers to reflect on material learned. With your students, create conversation, math, book, and even homework journals. Use focus free-writes to solicit impromptu writing from students in direct relationship to something that has occurred in the classroom. For example, after reading a novel, watching a video, experiencing a field trip, or listening to a guest speaker, ask students to do a timed writing. (You should also write during this time.) The rule is: write continually during the time period. (I set the timer for seven minutes.) After the timer has sounded, share responses. You and your students will marvel at everyone's insights. Save these responses in your teacher portfolio binder. End workshop periods by asking the question: "What did we just learn?" Never assume you know what students are learning. Always ask them (and yourself) to reflect.

EXPLORE YOUR CURRICULUM

F irst-grade teachers have a wonderful opportunity to engage children in some of their very first explorations of the school curriculum. It is in the first-grade classroom that science, social studies, math, and literacy combine to create whole new worlds of learning. But in order to prepare and excite students for learning for this year and beyond, teachers need to provide meaningful, hands-on experiences. This chapter will help you do just that!

Language Arts Instruction

The Balanced-Literacy Approach

Students in first grade need to have many experiences in the language arts as they grow to become independent readers and writers. Current research emphasizes the importance of using a balanced-literacy approach to ensure that your students become skilled in this area. Gay Su Pinnell and Irene Fountas discuss this concept in their book *Guided Reading: Good First Teaching for All Children.*

A balanced-literacy program falls into these eight categories:

1. **Read-Aloud**
   Story Time: model and teach reading skills from the point of view of the reader (whole or small group). Use
   - picture books
   - novels
   - factual books
   - poetry

2. **Shared Reading**
   Whole-group and small-group instruction: a shared experience used to practice (and play!) with language, model fluency, and teach reading skills in context. Use
   - big books
   - poetry on charts
   - songs

3. **Guided Reading**
   Small-group instruction based on text-level expertise: teacher-directed guidance for the reading process. Use
   - multiple copies of same text
   - single copies of leveled text

4. Independent Reading

Individual reading of known text and text at instructional level of the reader. Use
- multiple copies of already-read text
- texts of similar levels
- literature circles

5. Interactive Writing

Whole- or small-group instruction led by the teacher: model and teach skills needed for language arts acquisition. Use
- minimal-cues messages
- news share
- proofreading exercises
- interactive charts
- lessons with dry-erase boards/magnetic letters
- word-wall activities

6. Shared Writing

Whole- or small-group instruction: teacher models the writing process. Use
- news share
- writing mini-lessons

7. Guided Writing

Whole-, small-, or one-on-one group instruction during the writing process. Convene
- writing mini-lessons
- content-setting conferences
- editing conferences

8. Independent Writing

Students write individually at their appropriate instructional level. They can do this through

- process-writing workshop
- conversation journals
- book-dialogue journals
- traveling-book journals
- Graffiti-Wall messages

As you can tell, literacy skills cannot be taught in one forty-five minute reading period a day! Rather, literacy activities should abound throughout your daily and weekly schedules.

Question & Answer

What are the other students doing while you are meeting with small groups or one-on-one with individual students?

The students and I review and practice each curriculum-area routine until they know exactly what is expected of them (e.g., work-related choices and behaviors) during this time. Only when students are comfortable with the routine will I add small-group instruction into our daily schedule. (See Chapter 2 for more on classroom routines. See "Center Management Board," page 114.)

What does the term language arts mean?

Language arts refers to the processes of reading, writing, speaking, and listening. Some school districts also include viewing, as our society has become so visual.

Reading Instruction

Read Aloud!

My all-time favorite time of the day (and the real reason I became a teacher!) is read-aloud time! I love reading to children, and this is the best time for teaching and modeling the skills and joys of reading to the class. During "read-alouds" I read longer, novel-length books to my Room 6 students. It is through these longer books that I model

- the joy of reading
- fluency of reading
- book language
- story grammar
- the skill of holding a book in your head
- the art of creating pictures in your mind
- techniques for reading and understanding different text genres

Read-aloud time is a shared literacy event and a very active portion of literacy instruction. During this time, engage your students in conversations about the book being read, predict what will happen next, and confirm your predictions as you read. At the start of each read-aloud time, ask the class to "recap" the last chapter you read. By doing this you are working with the entire class on the techniques of "retelling" a story. Retellings are a great way to assess how much students actually comprehend when they read.

Below is a list of books I recommend for your class during read-aloud time:

- *James and the Giant Peach*, Roald Dahl (Penguin)
- *The Canada Geese Quilt*, Natalie Kinsey-Warnock (Bantam Doubleday Dell Publishing Group)
- *The Castle in the Attic*, Elizabeth Northrop (Bantam Doubleday Dell Books for Young Readers)
- *The Battle for the Castle*, Elizabeth Northrop (Bantam Doubleday Dell Books for Young Readers)
- *The Grand Escape*, Phyllis Reynolds Naylor (Bantam Doubleday Publishing Group)
- *Shiloh*, Phyllis Reynolds Naylor (Simon and Schuster)
- *Junie B. Jones* (series), Barbara Park (Random House)
- *Time Warp Trio* (series), John Scieszka (Viking Children's Books)
- *Catwings* (series), Ursula LeGuin (Orchard Books)
- *My Father's Dragon* (series), Ruth Stiles Gannet (Random House)

Shared Reading

Shared reading is a great time for students to "play" with language, an exercise that will help them become fluent readers. Fluency is best built when children have ample opportunities to read text that is familiar and easy for them. They need to be able to read the text independently so they can work on how it should "sound" to others. Think about it—do you consider yourself to be a fluent reader when you are reading a chemistry textbook? Children need to be able to roll language around on their tongue, making use of the rhyme and cadence of the words and sentences they are reading.

I recommend you use lots of poetry, as the visual images and vocabulary in poems are usually challenging, but because they are contained in a short amount of text (depending on the poem) they appear more manageable. (I recommend you enlarge the text you are currently reading with your class onto chart paper so the entire class can read along while you instruct.) Sing these poems. Clap them. Act them out. Teach skills to your children through these wonderful shared experiences, which foster

- phonemic awareness
- vocabulary development
- sight vocabulary
- rhyming patterns
- spelling patterns
- phonics skills
- reading fluency

To make these lessons even more fun, take them "on the road" to share with other classrooms. Presenting in front of an audience encourages students to do their best and rise to higher levels of learning. It helps give meaning to their work.

Below is a list of my favorite poets. Not only do they write beautiful, comical, and thoughtful verse, they also write poems that align with my thematic studies, which allows me to teach two things at once!

Check out poetry by:
- Jack Prelutsky
- Myra Cohn Livingston
- Brod Bagert
- Jane Yolen
- Shel Silverstein
- Paul Fleischman

I often make books for my children using the poems we are studying. During our medieval unit, for example, I bound together a collection of our favorite dragon poems, which students then brought home to share with their families. This made students feel proud, as they could share confidently their reading and language skills.

Poetry Books

Send poetry books home for children to read to their parents once students can read all the poems successfully. Students can illustrate the books and sometimes fill in the rhyming words as a cloze activity. Because the students already know the poems, this assignment tends to be stress free and fun, a chance for each child to show off his/her learning with confidence and authority!

When the students arrive at school the next day, have them add the name of that family member to whom they read to a classroom poetry graph. Keep a stack of cards for students to write on, and set the graph up with the names of the poems written across the bottom. Students can now write their family member's name on the card and place it in the pocket chart above the name of that person's favorite poem. (Since each child wants to be part of the graph, they are enthusiastic about completing their homework!)

This graph can now become part of your math-talk later in the day. For example, you might discuss which poem received the most votes; which poem received the fewest; how many the class received total; what the difference is between the number of votes the most popular poem received and the number of votes the least popular received.

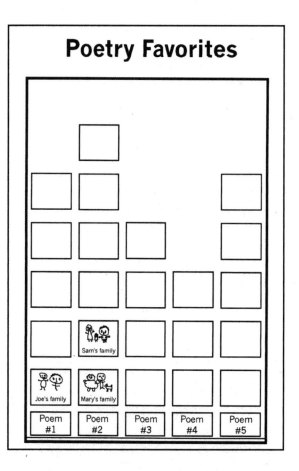

Name: _____ **Date:** _____

Poetry Homework

Read your book of poetry to someone in your family.

Who listened to you read? _____

Which poem was your favorite? _____

You can keep your poetry book at home, but bring this paper back to school.
  Add the name of your favorite poem to our classroom graph.

- -

Name: _____ **Date:** _____

Poetry Homework

Read your book of poetry to someone in your family.

Who listened to you read? _____

Which poem was your favorite? _____

You can keep your poetry book at home, but bring this paper back to school.
  Add the name of your favorite poem to our classroom graph.

Reproducible

Guided Reading

The term "guided reading"—the process of guiding students through text—was coined by Gay Su Pinnell and Irene Fountas. The concept has actually been in practice for quite some time, it's just that teachers have not always been as direct as they could have been with the actual teaching of the three cueing systems: graphophonic, semantic, and syntactic.

Guided reading is a supported social reading experience that takes the best of what has been learned through the *Reading Recovery* program—where students are taught one-on-one—and helps make it manageable for groups of students within a real classroom setting. Guided reading works best with small groups of students.

With guided reading instruction*:
- Students develop as individual readers while working in a socially supported activity
- Teachers observe students as they process new texts
- Individual students develop reading strategies so they can read increasingly difficult text independently
- Students enjoy successful experiences while reading for meaning
- Students develop those skills (e.g., use of the three cueing systems—graphophonic, semantic, syntactic; picture clues; prediction; and visualization of text) necessary for independent reading
- Students develop the means by which to introduce texts to themselves

Children are ready for guided reading when they can
- control left-to-right directionality
- understand one-to-one matching
- differentiate between words and letters
- control prominent consonant sounds
- locate an unknown work using initial/final-letter cues

Guided reading allows you to place your students into flexible groups, to use trade books, anthologies, or basal readers for instruction, and to observe and assess your students. But for this system to be successful, you need to know each student's reading ability, as you want them to read the text with ninety percent accuracy, which you can determine through using benchmark books with running records). Students will eventually read at 100 percent accuracy through the guided reading lesson.

What are your other students doing while you are working in a guided reading group? Depending on the amount of activity and noise you want in the room, this is a perfect time for students to either work in the learning centers or read independently. Set up a system that allows students to be engaged in language arts activities while you are working with your guided reading group. You might choose to use a center management board (see page 114) or a contract system (see page 99) to help manage this task. (See "Reading Workshop," page 40, for additional ideas.)

* Summarized with permission from: Guided Reading: Good First Teaching for All Children, *by Irene C. Fountas and Gay Su Pinnell. Copyright © 1996 by Irene C. Fountas and Gay Su Pinnell. Published by Heinemann, a division of Reed Elsevier, Inc., Portsmouth, New Hampshire. www.heinemann.com.*

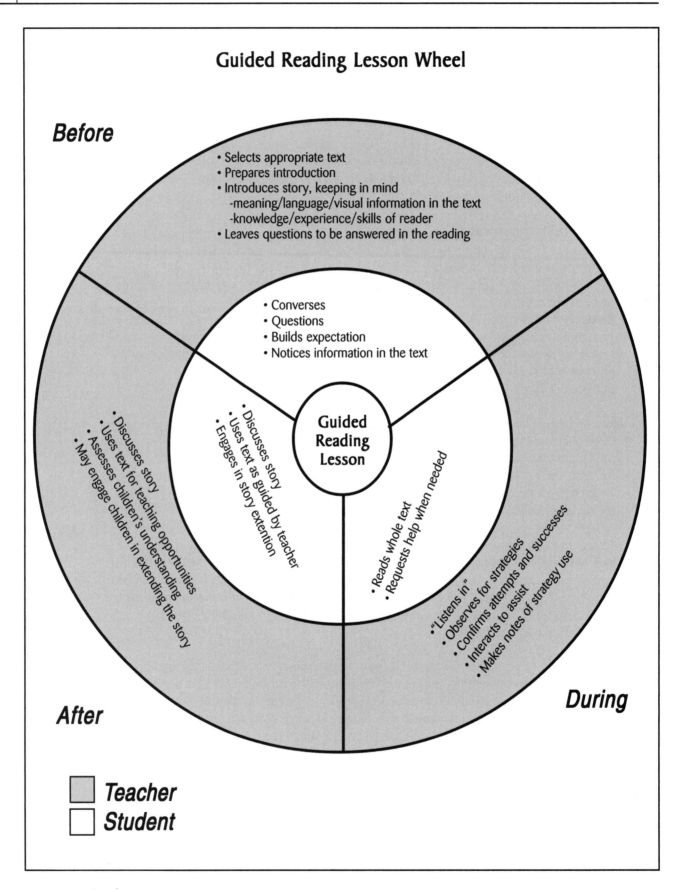

Guided Reading Lesson Wheel

Before

• Selects appropriate text
• Prepares introduction
• Introduces story, keeping in mind
   -meaning/language/visual information in the text
   -knowledge/experience/skills of reader
• Leaves questions to be answered in the reading

• Converses
• Questions
• Builds expectation
• Notices information in the text

• Discusses story
• Uses text as guided by teacher
• Engages in story extention

Guided
Reading
Lesson

• Reads whole text
• Requests help when needed

• Discusses story
• Uses text for teaching opportunities
• Assesses children's understanding
• May engage children in extending the story

• "Listens in"
• Observes for strategies
• Confirms attempts and successes
• Interacts to assist
• Makes notes of strategy use

During

After

Teacher
Student

Question & Answer

What do you mean by a contract?

Include a contract in each student's work folder. Contracts should include spaces for four or five centers.

The student "contracts" to complete these centers and meets with you once s/he has finished the assigned activities.

Together, the student and teacher can select the next activities.

Remember to teach center activities and clearly explain center expectations before students begin contracts. This will help ensure a more successful time block for everyone.

Contract for Independent Language Arts Time

Date _____

I, _____, agree to complete the following activities to the best of my abilities:

1. _____

2. _____

3. _____

4. _____

5. _____

Date Completed: _____

_____
Official Signature

GOAL Getter

Independent Reading

Children should have lots of opportunities to read independently. In Room 6 I always save a short block of time each day for U.S.S.R.—Uninterrupted Sustained Silent Reading—an acronym coined by a favorite professor of mine at the University of Vermont, Dr. Lyman C. Hunt Jr. Dr. Hunt believes that if we want to create real readers, teachers need to set aside time exclusively dedicated to independent reading—reading just for the pure joy of it! During U.S.S.R. the students and the teacher read whatever they want. It is important for the teacher to read (and I don't mean read an instruction manual, I mean read a real novel!) so that s/he models reading to his/her class. Children love to know what their teacher is reading for pleasure!

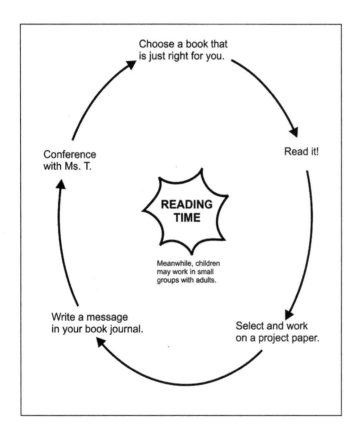

Choose a book that is just right for you.

Read it!

Conference with Ms. T.

READING TIME

Meanwhile, children may work in small groups with adults.

Write a message in your book journal.

Select and work on a project paper.

Reading Time Routine

I suggest you also set up a reading workshop time to help you manage the differing needs of your student readers. I prefer a quiet room when I work with reading groups, yet I also want those students who are working independently to be participating in lots of literacy activities, which, of course, would undoubtedly produce noise. To solve this dilemma, I created a routine for our reading time, which allows students to read quietly while I meet with my guided reading groups or one-on-one with students for conferences. I save the more active, "noisier" language arts activities for Free-Choice Time, as there is naturally more movement during that block. (See page 36 for the step-by-step Reading Time Routine procedure; see page 72 for Book Conference Tally reproducible.)

Question & Answer

What does "workshop" mean in Room 6?

I use the word "workshop" to designate times when students work in a particular curriculum area—language arts, for instance. Workshop times are open-ended, as students are always "in the process" of reading or responding to a book. A workshop format allows students to work at their own ability level and at their own pace.

Writing Instruction

If children are to become independent writers, they will need plenty of experience with the writing process. To help foster the necessary skills in each of your students, follow these three instructional techniques:

1. Interactive Writing
2. Shared Writing
3. Guided Writing
4. Independent Writing

Interactive Writing

Interactive writing is a fun and instructive way to make the writing process real and meaningful for you and your students. A wonderful and informative resource on this program is *Interactive Writing: How Language and Literacy Come Together* (K–2), by Gay Su Pinnell, Irene Fountas, and Andrea McCarrier.

During interactive writing, the teacher and students share the task of writing (you actually share the writing utensil with your students). Writing is a group event, which should take place at an easel or a chart stand. In this process, the teacher helps his/her students articulate individual letter sounds as they create the written text together. This mutual endeavor requires lots of talk and encouragement as you guide students through the writing process.*

Discuss with your class each of the following areas, as outlined in *Interactive Writing: How Language and Literacy Come Together* (K–2), during your interactive writing time. Helping students understand the process will aid them in becoming better writers.

- Experiencing: Engage your students in a conversation about something they have experienced—a favorite story, a field trip, or a movie. Discover what their interests are.

- Conversing: Discuss why people write, what people write about, and why.

- Composing: Decide what you want to write about. Brainstorm and list ideas.

- Constructing: At this stage you and your students are actively engaged in the writing process. Listen to and try out different words and letter sounds. Here, the writing utensil changes hands between teacher and students.

- Rereading: Throughout the process, students should pause from actual writing and reread what they have written. This allows them to review and reinforce the writing process.

- Summarizing: Focus conversation on what was learned.

- Revisiting: Revisit the text once finished. Display writing in a visible location so students can continue to add details and review grammar and punctuation.

- Extending: Continue adding to and revising the text. This teaches the importance of revision.

Keep in mind that the power of interactive writing lies in the process, not just the following of steps to get to a finished product. It is the conversation and the enthusiasm students and teachers bring to the writing process that gives interactive writing its benefits as a teaching tool.

* *Summarized with permission from:* Interactive Writing: How Language and Literacy Come Together (K-2), *by Andrea McCarrier, Irene C. Fountas, and Gay Su Pinnell. Copyright © 2000 by Andrea McCarrier, Irene C. Fountas, and Gay Su Pinnell. Published by Heinemann, a division of Reed Elsevier, Inc., Portsmouth, New Hampshire. www.heinemann.com.*

Minimal-Cues Messages

Minimal-cues messages help teach students some very powerful attributes important to the reading/writing process. Our best messages are related to the books we read together as a class. Often the messages are in the form of a question, and once they are solved we then take the time to discuss them, at which point I ask students to predict why this particular message was chosen.

Here's what to do:

1. Write messages (using blanks) as you would for Hangman.

2. Leave blanks for word letters, and group blanks together into phrases or sentences.

3. Guide students through mini-discussions about the message and how they can solve it.

4. Teach reading strategies such as *prediction, reading on*, and *trying again*. Through it all, students are actively involved in the meaning-making of the message. Each of their individual skills can and does shine through as the group problem-solves the message.

Example:

\- \- \-   \- \- \- \- \- \- \-   \- \- \- \- \-   \- \- \- \- \- \-   \- \-   \- \- \- \-   \- \-   \- \- \-

\- \- \- \- \- \- \- \- \- \- ‘\-   \- \- \- \- \- \- \- \- \- \-,   \- \-   \- \- \- \- \-   \- \- \- \- \- \-.

5. Ask the class to read the message together first.

6. Ask: "What do you know about the message?" Students should note the number of words, the number of sentences, punctuation, etc. Much discussion can be derived from this most minimal of minimal-cues messages before any words are even discovered!

7. Next, the students begin to solve the message. Ask them to note the placement of their prediction, giving a whole-word clue. That is, they may say, "I would like the word *the* for the first row, first word." I would respond, "That's right. How would that word begin?" Students respond, "With a capital T." "Why?" I would ask. "It is the beginning of a sentence," they would answer. How would you write *the*?" I would ask. "What letters make that sound?"

8. Next, ask the question, "Can you solve the message now?" Students will know that the word *the* is not powerful enough to help them solve it. They realize they will need the context of the message to help them do this.

As the message is filled in, we read it aloud. This gives the students many opportunities to predict text and to practice those skills used by more flexible, strategic readers. If the class gets stuck in the message and cannot go on, I let them "buy" a vowel and a consonant to help with the process of discovering the message.

(Answer to the message: The Newbery Award winner for 1996 is *The Midwife's Apprentice*, by Karen Cushman.)

Note: Many classroom teachers use minimal-cues messages, but they keep some letters in their message. For example, if they are working on vowel sounds in the class, their message might look like this:

G - - d   m - - n - ng   cl - ss.

In interactive writing:
- Children can be grouped based on learning goals.
- The writing is for real reasons.
- The task of writing is shared.
- Talk supports the process.
- The group creates a common text.
- The writing makes use of print conventions.
- Students and teacher make letter-sound connections.
- Students make overt connections between reading and writing.
- Teachers directly teach the writing process.

Use interactive writing any time you think sharing the writing process will help your students learn more. In the end, active participation will teach more than passive seat work!

Use interactive writing for:
- morning message
- minimal-cues messages
- extending a shared story
- summarizing a shared story
- writing out a survey question for students to answer
- writing a letter to an individual or another class
- recording information from an inquiry project/theme-study
- adding to or summarizing a guided reading lesson story

Shared Writing

Shared writing is a wonderful tool for teaching literacy skills to first graders, plus it provides great opportunities to really get to know the students in your classroom. In Room 6 I use Today's News to model the writing process and teach literacy skills. It is a favorite time for us all, one in which we get to know each other a little better.

To begin Today's News, gather your class at a common meeting spot. Use 18" x 24" white construction paper to write on. This paper is large enough to gather quite a bit of news but not too large to make the session drag. Remember, these are first graders! Besides, not everyone needs to share every day. Take this time to emphasize the important lesson of taking turns.

Now, ask if anyone has any news to share, and write down, verbatim, exactly what the contributing student tells you, trying to stay true to his/her language, changing from first person to third person, of course. Chat with the student, solicit more information, and ask clarifying questions in an effort to model the importance of questioning and clarifying (this also keeps the news interesting for the other students). Talk and write at the same time, and don't forget to share stories about yourself.

As I write each child's message I alternate the marker color, creating a pattern within the message. When the paper is full, I ask the children, "Does anyone know my pattern?" The pattern question causes the children to focus their attention on the print, at which time I ask them a focus question. For example, perhaps the text has compound words or several words with plural endings. Together, we answer queries with examples from our shared writing.

Shared writing is also a nice way for the teacher and students to exchange more information about themselves, building a stronger classroom community.

Question & Answer

How do you know what questions to ask for Today's News?

I use my school district's language arts curriculum to guide my questions. I center my questions on skills that help highlight word structure, grammar, and spelling. I keep track of the skills I have taught on a strip of paper, which hangs right next to the Today's News sheet. Now, other teachers, my administrator, and parents can see what I have been teaching my students.

Today's News allows you to model the writing process and teach a skill lesson that students will need in future reading and writing situations. I do not test students on the news or the skills we discussed, nor do I require them to copy it down. I do, however, check for their understanding of the writing process in their own independent writing.

Guided Writing and the Writing Process

Guided writing instruction happens in much the same way as guided reading instruction: the teacher instructs the student during the actual writing process. *In the Middle New Understandings About Writing, Reading, and Learning*, by Nancie Atwell, is an informative, highly readable resource. Atwell's book explains writers workshop and how interrupting students while they are writing in order to instruct them (then letting them get back to their own writing process to actually put the skill into use) is all part of the guided writing process.

Students need to understand the whole process if they are to become strategic writers. Below is the writing process, as outlined in *Interactive Writing: How Language and Literacy Come Together* (K–2). Use this basic instruction to teach your whole group mini-lessons as you begin your workshop time.*

- Purpose: a writer needs a reason for writing.

- Audience: a writer needs to think about who will be reading his/her writing.

- Form: with the purpose and the audience in mind, the writer needs to consider what form his/her writing should take.

- Composition: a writer needs to make use of print conventions while constructing his/her message.

- Reflection: as a writer writes, s/he reads and rereads the message, considering each part in the context of the whole message, thus editing and revising the final product as s/he continues writing.

- Layout: a writer needs to consider how the text will be placed on the paper, always thinking about the audience and what techniques will make the writing clearer.

In Room 6 I tend to guide the writing process through small-group mini-lessons. Often the mini-lesson is based on a particular need exhibited in all the students' writing (e.g., incorrect usage of punctuation), or it may be based on a pattern of need seen in just a few students' writing. I use mini-lessons to present new types of writing formats and extend the proficiency of the writers. Much of my language arts curriculum is taught through these mini-lessons, so there is little need for worksheets when students can use the lesson right in their own writing!

I also set up a conference structure within my writers workshop time that requires students to talk with at least two different people before a piece of writing is even considered for publication. These conferences cover several important aspects of the process in which the students
- involve one or two classmates in their writing
- share their current writing piece out loud
- participate in a peer conference
- complete a peer-conference sheet (see sample conference sheet, page 83)

* Summarized with permission from: Guided Reading: Good First Teaching for All Children, by Irene C. Fountas and Gay Su Pinnell. Copyright © 1996 by Irene C. Fountas and Gay Su Pinnell. Published by Heinemann, a division of Reed Elsevier, Inc., Portsmouth, New Hampshire. www.heinemann.com.

Independent Writing

Independent writing happens throughout the day, takes many forms, and allows students to use the writing process at their own developmental level. By giving a variety of writing experiences, students begin to make the new teaching their own. Another plus is that very few worksheets are necessary, as there are so many other ways, as listed below, to provide for real writing practice.

Writing Time Routine

When preparing students for their independent workshop time, I teach them a routine for the time block. As they learn each step on the routine and begin to feel real ownership of the time, I start holding conferences and small-group lessons, as I know everyone understands exactly what is expected of them.

With your class, develop your own routine and adjust it as the year progresses. Once students learn the routine, the workshop begins to take on a life of its own.

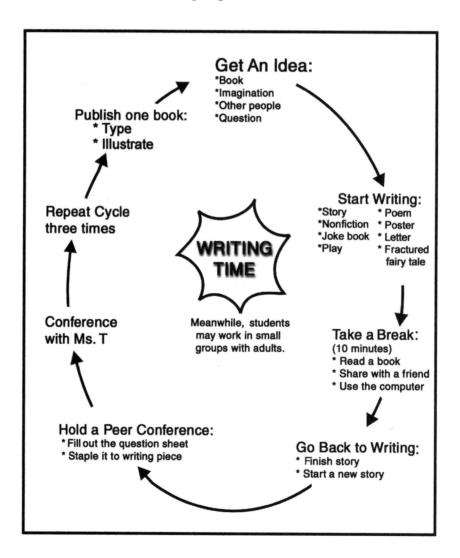

During this workshop time, my conferences with students fall into two categories: content setting and editing. In a content-setting conference, students share their written story with me. I ask questions and offer suggestions I think will make the student's story more complete. An editing conference occurs only after a student has decided to publish a piece of his/her writing. In Room 6 students do not publish every piece of their writing. They usually write three pieces and choose one of these three to bring to final form for an audience. The number of books they publish per term varies from student to student, but each student publishes six or more books a year. It is during this editing conference that I try to articulate to the student parts of the process that s/he can do on his/her own. I also use this time to teach a new skill the student is starting to develop in his/her writing. In other words, I show this student a "next step," just as we do in a guided reading situation. Build on what is already known and help students identify connections for new learning.

At each of these conferences I take notes for myself and for the student about what s/he can do and what s/he needs to work on. Students keep this list in their writing folder as a reminder of individual expectations. (See page 73 for the Writing Conference Tally reproducible.)

Journals

In Room 6 I incorporate journal writing into every curriculum area. Most of my journals are written in dialogue fashion: I write a message back to the child, modeling the writing process for each student. Below are a few of the journals we use in Room 6:

- **Conversation Journals:** Conversation journals allow the teacher to get to know his/her students better and, conversely, let students get to know their teacher on a more personal level. Messages might include what you did over the weekend, books you are reading, activities you do with your family. These journals require daily communication between the student and the teacher.

- **Book Dialogue Journals:** These journals are ongoing conversations between the student and the teacher about the books the student has read or is currently reading.

- **Math Journals:** Students use these to keep various records during math time. They also note what skills they are practicing and learning. After a math conference students leave their journals with me for my response.

- **Homework Journals:** Students keep homework journals to list homework assignments. This also helps parents keep track of what's being taught in the classroom. I collect and comment on these journals once a week.

A Peek Inside Room 6

Conversation Journal Center

Materials

- Small journals (e.g., assignment notebooks)
- Writing implements: pencils, markers, crayons
- Reader/Writer: usually an adult (teacher, volunteer, older student). As students gain more reading skills, they can read independently.
- Date stamp/stamp pad: available at most stores that sell school/office supplies

Directions

Students get their journal and, with the aid of an older reader, "read" the message their teacher wrote. Students are then encouraged to write back, using letters, words, or pictures. They finish their entry by stamping the date on the journal page.

Next, students share their writing with an adult at the center. The adult jots down the message on a Post-It® note and sticks it to the entry in order to help the teacher decipher the beginning writers' messages. Finally, the teacher responds to the journal, often making use of the child's own language, and places it back in the journal bin.

Note: Students should keep journals throughout the year as a record of their growth as writers. These journals help inform the teacher as to the progress individual students are making and alert him/her to patterns occurring in the development of classroom writers. Journals, therefore, become a catalyst for future literacy lessons. These journals produce a visual record of growth and should be shared with parents at conferences and other meetings.

Graffiti Wall

Another fun independent writing activity is the Graffiti Wall, a place on which students can write impromptu messages to each other or respond to a message written by the teacher. To set up this message board, just leave space on a bulletin board or the back of an easel (one covered in cork board) and label it "Graffiti Wall." Push pins, small pieces of writing paper, and writing utensils are all you need to get this started. Your students will do the rest! (I love to leave messages for the class on the Graffiti Wall and gather their responses. Some years my students and I collect the wall items to make an album of class writing. Students love to review their notes!)

Keyword Time

Keyword, a term coined by Jeanette Veatch and based on research by Sylvia Ashton Warner (*Teacher*), has become part of a favorite learning time. Here's how Keyword Time works in Room 6:

In my room Keyword Time occurs one day a week, although students may opt to do this activity during Free-Choice Time. During Keyword Time, students choose for themselves a word to have as their very own. This word is not necessarily from a book or a word wall—it is whatever word they are interested in. When they have chosen the word, they tell me about the word and I write it on an index card for them. As I write down the word I stretch it out and, individually, have each student interact with the writing of the word (e.g., say the word, spell the word, state what letter the word begins with). The student then takes his/her word back to his/her work area, illustrates the word, then writes using that word on a classroom-ready form that allows room for both text and illustration. The word should be spelled correctly, but the rest of the writing can look more "kid-like." Expectations for how much a student writes are established beforehand with me.

Students keep their words on a word ring (simply hole punch the upper left-hand corner of the index card and slide onto ring). Organizing key words on index cards gives students the freedom to easily sort their words. It allows the teacher to have the students work with their words in order to put together word sorts based on skills being learned in the words in print. First graders will often find words later that belong in a certain category and, therefore, will need to add or change their choice, so writing them on index cards helps. Having children sort their cards allows the teacher to quickly see who understands the activity and who needs more assistance. Students can now easily use these words any time during the day to help them get ideas or prompt their writing.

Children meet with me individually to share their writing from their previous word and to share with me what their new word will be. For beginning readers, point out the beginning sound. For intermediate readers, focus on the middle of the word (vowels, double consonants, etc.). And for skilled readers, discuss a particular spelling pattern associated with the chosen word. These are the "miniest" of mini-lessons. When each student has written about ten words, s/he can brainstorm a title and put together a book, stapling construction paper on for the front and back covers. This simple book, along with published trade books and our own books produced during writing workshop time, becomes part of our classroom library. Keep in mind this was a very personal time in which students were not grouped.

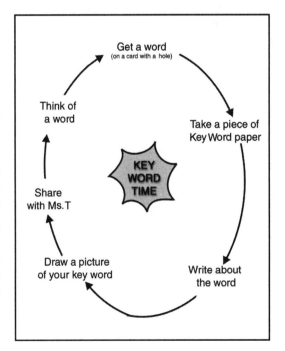

Every week or so, we hold a special Keyword Time. On these days I teach a specific skill to the entire class, using each student's word as the basis for the group lesson. (I usually ask the class to gather at the story chair with their favorite keywords.) Now I have twenty-plus words with which to illustrate a variety of lessons—alphabetical order, number of syllables, vowel sounds, and parts of speech. Later in the year, on another special Keyword day, the students are in charge of the lesson. During this time they form small groups, share their words with one another, then sort them alphabetically. Much later in the year, when students' word collections have grown, they might, on their own, sort their words alphabetically. Because they are using their own personal words, and not a teacher's arbitrary list, they are more apt to engage in the activity—ultimately understanding the concept at a higher level.

When our special Keyword lesson is completed, students start the routine again, writing and illustrating their words.

My favorite type of lesson, however, is when each student chooses his/her own method for sorting and then asks one or more of their classmates to guess how s/he sorted them. Each student records the sorting method using a ready-made form designed especially for this exercise.

Weekly Spelling Challenge: "I Almost Know How to Spell" Words

Weekly Spelling Challenge is a homework assignment that I recommend students and parents work on no earlier than the second grading quarter. Here's how it works: With each student, choose five words s/he can almost spell correctly. Record these words in the right-hand column of the Weekly Spelling Challenge reproducible (see page 111). Students now take this sheet home to practice writing words with his/her parents. At some point during the week, students should bring this list back into school and sign up for an individual spelling test, also called a "Spelling Check-In." If students are still having trouble with particular spellings add these to their next list of words they need to practice. They can then take a new list home to practice that contains both their old and new words, or they can practice their list at school during spelling workshop time. This exercise is great for penmanship practice, too. And at some point you might consider requesting students write their words in alphabetical order.

Weekly Spelling Challenge

Name: _____ Date: _____

Your child has chosen 5 words from his/her personal writing that s/he would like to know how to spell correctly. The homework challenge is to help your child practice these words during the school week at home. We will have lots of special times to practice them at school, also. During the week your child will sign up for a spelling check-in for these words. If your child has learned them, the new words will be chosen. Words that still need work will remain on the list. Our goal is to create spellers who care about spelling in their work— a spelling attitude, if you will!

Words to spell correctly	Practice	Practice
1.		
2.		
3.		
4.		
5.		

Language Arts Ideas for Your Literacy Centers

During spelling workshop, students may either practice words or work in literacy centers. Below are some of the centers we use in Room 6:

Print Hunt: Have several pointers available for students to use as they point and read all of the print in the classroom. I usually keep a container of four or five pointers. When the container is empty it indicates that the "center" is full. This open-ended activity changes as you change the print in the room. (See page 21 for more information on "Print Hunt.")

Word Play: Keep magnetic letters and words available for your students to read, sort, and combine into words and sentences. But first, teach different types of activities to the class, then, require the children to perform them independently at this center. Activities change based on your whole-class explorations and the addition of new vocabulary words.

"I Can Read" Box: Store all the books that students have read during a guided reading lesson in this box. Students can now go to the "I Can Read" box to revisit familiar stories.

Poems: Create poem cards by mounting copies of your charts on tag board. Laminate. Children can read these independently.

Computer Programs: Keep a language arts program on the classroom computer(s) for students to experiment with. Using the computer helps improve fine-motor, computer, and language arts skills.

Games: Games are a great way to reinforce material and skills. Keep a variety of phonics and sight vocabulary games in the classroom for students to choose from. Teach game rules to the entire class first, then, let students use them during independent playtime.

Buddy Read: "Buddy reading" allows students to practice all sorts of literacy skills, including pronunciation, enunciation, emphasis, and listening. A fun twist to this activity was shared with me by a teacher: Have each child make an 18" paper doll "buddy." Use crayons or construction paper to make them colorful. Laminate. Now, hang these "buddies" low to the ground along the classroom wall. When children want to "buddy read," they can read to their very own buddy!

Overhead Projector: Plug your overhead projector in so it shines on an open space on one of your classroom walls, making a small projection. Make available poem and short story transparencies. Students can project the text and read it with a friend or by themselves. (See page 60 for more information on the use of overhead projectors.)

Elbow Pipe Readers: Students will love this fun activity! Purchase several PVC elbow pipes (that's right, the type you find under your bathroom sink!). These pipes are shaped like telephones, and when students hold one to their ear and mouth, they create a mini-telephone into which they can read and out of which they can hear what they sound like! Keep four or five in the room. The student picks a just-right book and reads it into the "telephone."

Free-Choice Time: During this time students can participate in a center of their choice.

Listening Center: Keep in store a selection of books-on-tape for children to read along with. Require students to record the title of the story along with a picture of their favorite part in a listening center journal.

Teaching Math Through Children's Literature

A Peek Inside Room 6

Classroom-Tested Math Curriculum Activities

The Grouchy Ladybug, by Eric Carle

Teach your students how to tell time by using Eric Carle's most popular book, *The Grouchy Ladybug.* This story takes place over the period of one day, and each page displays a clock face that indicates the time of day and the rising/setting stage of the sun as the ladybug travels throughout the land.

After reading this book one year, Room 6 students decided to write and illustrate a big book similar to *The Grouchy Ladybug.* Because the focus of our yearlong theme-study was the rainforest, we changed the main character from a ladybug to a lizard. Students worked in pairs to construct each illustration—modeled after Eric Carle's painted paper and collage technique—of the newly rewritten story. Each pair created their clock face to represent the hour on each of the pages. I supplemented this by directly teaching the parts of a clock and how to tell time by the hour, half hour, and quarter hour. To assist in this teaching, I used a clock face with movable hands.

Once the big book was completed, each student made his/her own "little" book, in which s/he was responsible for creating all the clock faces used in the original story. Students illustrated their "little" books with markers and crayons.

Finally, each student read his/her own copy until s/he felt s/he could read it fluently to another person. At this point, each student created his/her own advertising poster and was "hired" by another classroom to read the book s/he had created. Of course, to get to appointments on time, each student had to read the classroom clock!

A Peek Inside Room 6

The Math and Literature Series

The math and literature series, contributed to, among others, by Marilyn Burns and Sylvia Fair, are wonderful resources for teaching math concepts. (Go to Math Solutions® Online, www.mathsolutions.com, to view series books).

One of my favorite books mentioned in this series is *The Bedspread* (William Morrow and Co.) by Sylvia Fair. This story involves two aging sisters who are as different as night and day from one another. When the sisters each find themselves confined to a bed, they decide to decorate a spread with a cloth rendition of the family home in which they grew up. One would think such a project would produce a symmetrical pattern, but due to the differences between the sisters' memories, they sew together a nonsymmetrical design instead.

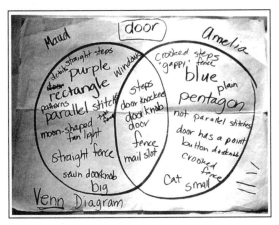

After the Room 6 students and I read *The Bedspread*, we noted the similarities and differences in the quilt by using a Venn diagram. I then had them create their own pictures, but we decided to draw castles instead of houses, as we were in the midst of a medieval theme-study. The students worked with partners, and at either end of a 12" x 18" sheet of paper (divided by a "wall" of folders), each partner drew a castle. The trick was they had to make the castles as similar as possible. Partners, therefore, had to talk with one another in order to draw symmetrical patterns.

After twenty minutes, the entire class lifted up their "walls" to view their partner's rendition. An audible sigh sounded around the room as they noticed how different or how similar their pictures were. As with *The Bedspread*, we used a Venn diagram to compare and contrast the various castles and their symmetries.

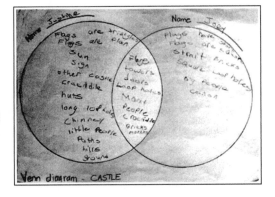

Small-Group Lessons and the Math Time Routine

Small-group lessons allow the teacher and students to explore complex concepts in greater detail. Work on problem-solving and computation strategies in your small groups, and encourage students to use various math games (see pages 119-123) during independent math time. Use the Math Time Routine to help manage students' activities.

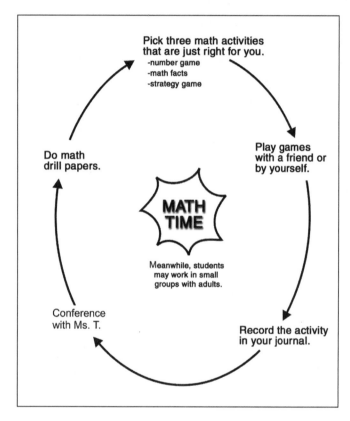

Math Games

A great game to use for beginning fraction work is Action Fraction! (Koplow Games, Inc., Boston, Massachusetts), in which students use pattern blocks as fraction manipulatives. I learned about this game through Rachel McAnallen, a Vermont teacher who is also the author of *Ms. Math Presents Action Fractions*.

Other games students can try are
• +3 Pathway (see page 119)
• Odd/Even Die Toss (see page 120)
• +, x, - Dice War (see page 121)
• Reach for 25 (see page 122)
• Mimic-a-Shape (see page 123)

Directions for these games appear on each game page. Acquaint yourself with each game first, then teach it, along with how to read the directions, to your students. Students will enjoy the various challenges, and you will appreciate the skills these games reinforce. These make great home-school activities, too!

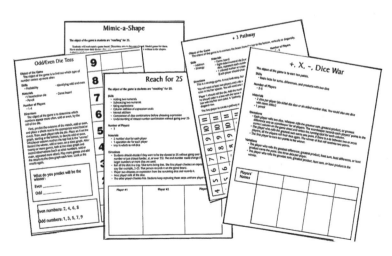

+ 3 Pathway

Object of the Game

The object of the game is to connect the boxes from the top to the bottom, vertically or diagonally.

Skills	Materials	Number of Players
• Addition • Strategy	• Game board • Eight-sided numeral die (numerals, not dots, represent each number) • 1 colored marker or crayon for each player (Each player should choose a different color.)	• 2-3

Directions

This is a strategy game. It may look easy, but it is challenging and often difficult to win.

You will need at least two players and a die with eight sides. Each player should have a marker or crayon to color in his/her spaces. You will need one game board to play.

Player 1 should roll the die. Add the number at the top of the game board (+3) with the number rolled. S/he should color in a box with the same number in it. Player 2 will proceed in the same manner, coloring a box with his/her own color. A "pathway" is formed when one player fills in all the squares in a vertical or diagonal row.

The first player to create a pathway is the winner!

4	5	6	7	8	9	10	11
4	5	6	7	8	9	10	11
4	5	6	7	8	9	10	11
4	5	6	7	8	9	10	11
4	5	6	7	8	9	10	11
4	5	6	7	8	9	10	11

Reproducible

Odd/Even Die Toss

Object of the Game

The object of the game is to find out which type of number comes up more often.

Skills

- Probability
- Identifying odd and even

Materials

- 1 hexahedron die
- Game board
- Pencil

Number of Players

- 1-4

Directions

First, predict the outcome of the match, odd or even, and place a check next to the appropriate word (odd or even). Then, each player rolls the die. Place an X on the graph, starting at the bottom, to denote odd or even. Whichever column reaches the top first is the "winner." Record the winner, odd or even, on a class graph. After twenty or more games, look at the class graph and record observations (such as what numbers, odd or even, appeared more often). Play more games and add the results to the class graph each time. Look at the results again.

What do you predict will be the winner:

Even _____

Odd _____

Even numbers: 2, 4, 6, 8

Odd numbers: 1, 3, 5, 7, 9

	Odd	Even
9		
8		
7		
6		
5		
4		
3		
2		
1		

+, x, -, Dice War

Object of the Game
   Earn ten points.

Skills
   • Basic facts for sums, differences, and products with two dice

Number of Players
   • 2-5

Materials
   • 2 dice per player (six-sided dot dice or six-sided number dice. You could also use dice with more sides.)
   • 1 pencil

Directions
   • Each player rolls two dice. Whoever rolls the greatest sum, greatest product, or greatest difference acts as scorekeeper for all players. The scorekeeper records each players' points in the correct column on the game sheet and writes the running total for each column.
   • The player who rolls the greatest sum earns one point. If there is a tie between two or more players, all the players roll their dice again. The winner of that roll receives two points.
   • The first player to earn ten points is the winner.

Variations
   • The player who rolls the greatest difference, greatest product, least sum, least difference, or least product earns the point. Use three dice per player.
   • The player who rolls the greatest sum, greatest product, least sum, or least product is the winner.

Players' Names				

Reach for 25

Object of the Game:
Reach for 25.

Skills
- Adding two numerals
- Subtracting two numerals
- Using expressions
- Column addition of expression totals
- Mental addition
- Comparison of dice combinations before choosing expression
- Understanding of closest number combination without going over 25

Number of Players
- 3

Materials
- 2 number dice for each player
- 1 operation die for each player
- Tray in which to roll dice

Directions
- Students should decide if they want to be the closest to 25 without going over this target number or just closest (under, at, or over 25). The end number could change if the dice with larger numbers or more dice are used.
- Roll all the dice in a tray. Take turns being first. The first player chooses an expression from the tray (for example, 2+3). That person records it on the game board.
- Player two chooses an expression from the remaining dice and records it.
- Next player rolls all the dice.
- The other player chooses first. Students keep repeating these steps until one player reaches 25.

Player #1	Player #2	Player #3

Mimic-a-Shape

Object of the Game:
- Students recognize shapes as fraction pieces
- Shapes, although they may look different, may carry some of the same properties

Skills
- Reinforces names of shapes
- Helps build self-esteem
- Encourages cooperative learning
- Helps students understand that while shapes may look different, they carry some of the same properties
- Helps students understand fractions
- Allows for more than one answer to be correct
- Introduces students to pre-algebra concepts

Materials
- Pattern blocks or pattern-block shapes (Reproducible pattern-block shapes are included on the top of each game board.)

Number of Players
- 2

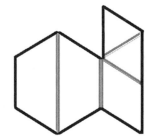

Player #1   2Z +1R+ 2T

Directions (for teacher to review with students)
Player 1 builds a shape using a handful of the pattern blocks or pattern-block shape reproducibles (shape designations: hexagon, trapezoid, rhombus, triangle). Once created, Player 1 traces the outside of his/her shape on a game board (piece of paper) and writes a number statement. In the visual example below, Player 1's larger shape is made up of the following smaller shapes: 2Z + 1R + 2T (2 Trapezoids + 1 Rhombus + 1 Triangle). Now, Player 2 looks at Player 1's outlined shape and uses his/her set of smaller shapes to build on top of Player 1's tracing. Note that Player 2 must use different smaller shapes to recreate Player 1's larger shape. For example, if Player 1 uses two trapezoids (2Z) to create a hexagon, Player 2, in order to also create a hexagon, uses instead one trapezoid (1Z) and 3 triangles (3T). The final number statement for Player 2 would be: 1Z + 3T + 2R (1 Trapezoid + 3 Triangles + 2 Rhombi). Player 2 has "mimicked" Player 1's shape using different shapes.

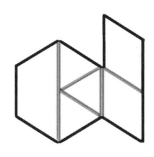

Player #2   1Z +3T+ 2R

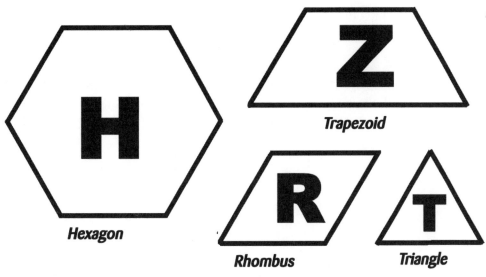

Hexagon

Trapezoid

Rhombus

Triangle

Question & Answer

How do you organize your math games?

I duplicate most of my math games on paper, allowing each student to select a game board of their choice for math choice time. I mount one copy of the game on the front of a file folder and laminate it (this makes duplicating easy!). I tape the two sides of the folder, making a pocket that can hold all the game board copies.

Bubble Gum Fun!

For teaching beginning measurement, no activity is more fun than a Bubble Gum Bubble Blowing Contest! Each fall I give Room 6 students a pack of bubble gum with which to chew and blow bubbles. Once the students start blowing bubbles, a partner or classroom volunteer measures the dimensions of each bubble.

To try this in your classroom, here's what to do: After students have finished blowing all the bubbles, gather back inside the classroom for a shared math lesson to compare measurement strategies, and record observations on chart paper. Students later share their observations and the different tricks they learned for measuring these explosive, sticky balloons.

Science Instruction

Scientific literacy implies that a person can identify scientific issues underlying national and local decisions and express positions that are scientifically and technologically informed. Therefore, students need to

observe,

learn about,

influence change, and

interact with the science that is all around them.

The principles guiding the National Science Education standards are:

- Science is for all students.
- Learning science is an active process.
- School science reflects the intellectual and cultural traditions that characterize the practice of contemporary science.
- Improving science education is part of systemic education reform.

Students in K–4 should develop the skills indicative of scientific inquiry, such as:

- Ask a question about objects, organisms, and events in the environment.
- Plan and conduct a simple investigation.
- Employ simple equipment and tools to gather data and extend the senses.
- Use data to conclude a reasonable explanation.
- Communicate investigations and explanations.

As teachers, we need to remember that the study of science encompasses many areas; it is important that we share each of these different sciences with students, including:

- Physical Science
- Life Science
- Earth and Space Science
- Science and Technology
- Science in Personal and Social Perspectives
- History and Nature of Science

The best science instruction in the first-grade classroom encourages students to ask their own questions while exploring in a hands-on environment. I suggest you set up whole-class demonstrations that inspire students to explore a concept further. These "Mr. Wizard" types of experiments, such as the Baking Soda and Vinegar Volcano (page 135), start with a bang and lead students to make exciting discoveries. (*Note*: For more information on Mr. Wizard, a.k.a., Don Herbert, go to: www.yesterdayland.com.)

Science and Your Classroom Theme

Reading, writing, and math lessons can easily be incorporated into your classroom theme-study; science explorations should be no different. This learning is powerful in that it allows students to see the interconnectedness of curriculum units with life itself.

In past years, I have been very fortunate to have instructional aides or parents lend a hand during science explorations. In order to assist them, I organize theme-related science mini-lessons for the aide or parent to share with the class during a free-choice time. These lessons are follow-ups to larger conceptual lessons the class and I are studying, and as part of the lesson, I require students to record vocabulary (see page 126) and keep notes in their science journals. These mini-lessons are instructive and fun, as they allow students to work in small groups with hands-on materials.

Have the following reproducible recording sheets on hand during a class or small group lesson. Once students have recorded key science vocabulary, these sheets can become part of their science journal.

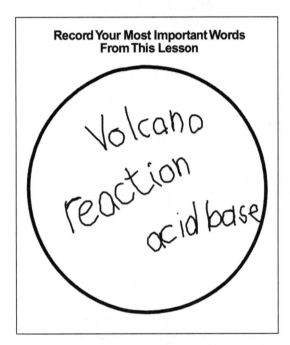

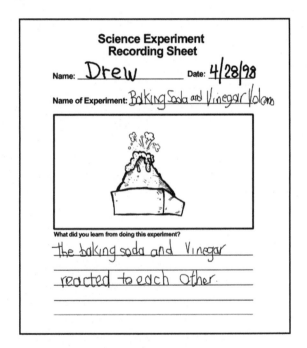

Why is this reproducible in the shape of a circle? Give yourself a needed break from listing words and allow students to complete this task by themselves. The circle shape is nice because it gives students a chance to write without having to worry about lines. Print this sheet on the back side of their "Science Experiment Recording Sheet," photocopy a number of these double-sided pages, and bind or staple into a personal science booklet for each student.

Students "draw" the steps to each experiment in the box provided. Beforehand, I teach them how to label each step, which they then turn into a picture. On the lines below the illustration box, students record their observations in note-taking or sentence form.

Record Your Most Important Words
From This Lesson

School Yard Square Recording Sheet

Directions:
Record three of your observations on this sheet. Share with your partner, then, share with the class!

I see _____.

I see _____.

I see _____.

Reproducible

Center Activity Ideas

"I See" Book: Have students create an "I See" book about their squares. They can illustrate objects they observed, use the sentence frames as their text to make into a ready-made blank book, and create a cover. Now they just have to share their books with the rest of the class. Students can also create one class book. Students simply choose one drawing from their three original "I See" drawings, which they can reproduce on a blank book page (see page 132 for reproducible). On the lines below the illustration box, students can write their observations. Now, just bind the individual pages together into a class "I See" book.

Bug Words: Purchase magnetic "bug" words for your science center. Have students sort magnets into two categories: "Words I Know" and "Words I Want to Know." Students can use these words to label a picture they have drawn on their "I See" page that shows who or what lives in their square. (*Note*: "Bug" words can be found at various locations— educational conferences, school supply catalogs, science stores. The particular kind I bought were produced by Fridge Fun! Inc., Santa Rosa, California. Check out the company's website: www.fridgefun.com.)

How Do Bugs See?: Place various lenses and objects at a center table. Ask the question: How do bugs see? Students can observe objects through the different lenses, note changes in the appearance of the objects with the different lenses, and describe these changes to a friend.

Nature Bingo: Have students make a Nature Bingo board, filling in each of the board squares with an object they observed in their school yard square. Students play Nature Bingo by going outside to their squares and checking off the objects as they see them. The first person to get three in a row is the winner. Students can also play so that the first person to find all of the objects is the winner. (See Nature Bingo reproducible, page 133.)

You can also make bingo boards by using the vocabulary generated by your students' observations. Drawings or magazine pictures can be used to create the boards, and word cards can be used for bingo calling cards.

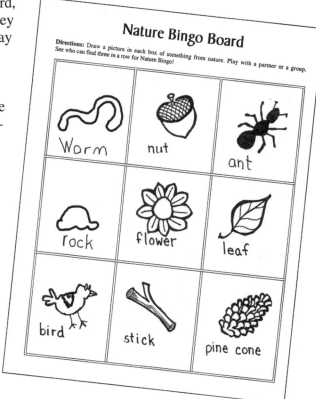

Nature Bingo Board

Directions: Draw a picture in each box of something from nature. Play with a partner or a group. See who can find three in a row for Nature Bingo!

Worm	nut	ant
rock	flower	leaf
bird	stick	pine cone

"I See"

I see

_____

_____

_____

Reproducible

Nature Bingo Board

Directions: Draw a picture in each box of something from nature. Play with a partner or a group. See who can find three things in a row for Nature Bingo!

Reproducible

Other Observation Activities

The following two activities may be different, but they both help strengthen important skills such as observation and prediction. Have students use the vocabulary and experiment recording sheets (pages 127 and 128, respectively) to note new words and discoveries. Once completed, students can add these pages to their science journals.

The Baking Soda and Vinegar Volcano

Students will enjoy making, "igniting," and observing this classroom-constructed volcano, and you will enjoy strengthening their direction-following, observation, and prediction skills through this fun, hands-on activity. See the reproducible on page 135 to see how this experiment works.

Observe a Snowflake

While not as explosive as the volcano, students will enjoy this activity nonetheless, and it will help strengthen their observation skills. See the reproducible on page 136 for more information.

Individual Goal Setting and Conference-Based Lessons

Individual goal setting and conference-based lessons give the teacher the opportunity to ask students, "What is it you want to learn next? What do you think you need to work on?" This type of mini-lesson places the child in charge of his/her learning, and it is an invaluable tool to the teacher as s/he listens to each student's version of what s/he is learning, what s/he wants to learn, and what s/he is comfortable doing. Take notes to help you better tailor your instruction to each student.

You might be surprised at how good students are at choosing goals for themselves. In fact, they often know exactly what the next logical step should be for themselves, and because it's their choice, they work even harder to meet their goals. In addition, these goals help direct their selections during their independent-choice time.

Baking Soda and Vinegar Volcano

Materials
- Plaster of paris or paper maché
- 1/4 cup baking soda
- 1/2 cup water
- 1/4 cup vinegar
- Six drops red food coloring
- One large soup can (empty)

Directions
- Mix plaster of paris or paper maché mixture according to directions.
- Build a volcano shape around the can with plaster of paris or paper maché and leave the open end of the can exposed.
- Paint the volcano in dark brown or gray colors.
- Mix the baking soda with food coloring in the volcano can.
- Slowly add vinegar.

Before adding the vinegar: What do you think will happen when you add the vinegar to the baking soda and water mixture?

After adding the vinegar: Draw a picture of what happened when you added the vinegar?

Why did that happen?

Observe a Snowflake

Snowflakes form when water vapor in the air condenses around a frozen drop of water called a crystal. Many small crystals of frozen water attach to each other, making snowflakes. The crystals attach together in such a manner that all snowflakes are six-sided or hexagonal, yet each snowflake is different from the other.

If you live where it snows, look closely at some snowflakes. When it first starts to snow big flakes, take a magnifying glass and a piece of black construction paper outdoors. With the magnifying glass, look closely at the individual flakes that land on the paper.

On the grid below, draw four snowflakes you observed. Try to draw what makes each of them unique.

USE THEMES TO ORGANIZE INSTRUCTION

First graders learn best when they make connections between new and prior knowledge, so it is not surprising that many first-grade teachers use thematic teaching as a basis for their instruction. Thematic teaching takes connections and uses them to enhance the learning in all subject areas—perfect for your students' developing minds!

Planning Your Theme-Study

Umbrella Themes

Most school districts require that teachers cover a specific curriculum. Your required topics are many, as are mine, so each year try to find the connections that will allow you to teach a yearlong theme-study.

Over the years I have determined I can easily group my science and social studies topics under what I call an "umbrella" theme. For example, I am required to teach about plants and animals. I could teach these subjects in two separate units—one about plants and one about animals—or I could consider a large "umbrella" theme—the rainforest—under which I would address both subject areas. The next year I will also address plants and animals, but I might teach them under the umbrella theme of the arctic. I am still teaching my basic curriculum, but I am able to reinvigorate the subject for me and my students by changing the setting for our discussions and, of course, the plants and animals! In short, creating an umbrella theme will allow teachers to teach the required subjects but to teach them differently each year, which will keep everyone excited and rejuvenated!

If you decide to use the umbrella-theme approach, once your umbrella theme is determined, explore your other curriculum strands (e.g., math, language arts, etc.), and ask yourself this important question: Will your theme exploration address standards and required curriculum while also allowing students to learn through real, hands-on, and meaningful experiences?

As you plan your theme, consider these points:

- Theme content: theme should not just be "cute." It should tap into your students' curiosity and help them answer real questions.
- Length of theme: extended themes will allow for more exploration and encourage more parent participation.
- Field trips: field trips to different places at different times of the day and year will enhance your theme-study.

- Learning opportunities: create real opportunities to share knowledge with others.
- Ownership: the students, the teacher, the parents, and the community should share ownership in the theme-study.
- Literature: an abundance of quality literature—fiction and nonfiction—should be provided and used.

Graphic Organizers

As you plan your theme-unit, use a graphic organizer to plot ideas. I am a great one for "webbing out" my first thoughts on paper. The computer doesn't work for me during this first step, as I need to get "messy" with these ideas. Once my thoughts are down on paper, I begin to organize them by finding connections. I then share my ideas with students and ask them for their input. Ultimately, a graphic organizer is born!

Create a Graphic Organizer in Five Easy Steps!

Our minds store knowledge in an organizational system known as schemas. Schemas are similar to graphic organizers in that they group information under a known heading. Any time a visual graphic is used to chart key ideas, the information becomes easier to remember. Teaching with graphic organizers, therefore, will help your students learn and remember more.

#1 Start with a Web
A web organizes your thoughts, questions, and/or topics while integrating curriculum areas. Webs can be teacher-generated or child-generated, although I strongly suggest teachers and students collaborate when creating the class theme-study web.

#2 Choose a Topic and Add the "Spokes" to Your Web
My class theme-study stems from a science or social studies concept that is required teaching for this grade level (e.g., the Middle Ages living in the Northeast weather, etc.).

- Write your theme in the middle of a large piece of paper. (See page 140 for a graphic organizer reproducible.)
- List subject areas around the exterior of the paper like the spokes in a wheel. Subject areas might include:

Writing	Reading
Math	Science
Social Studies	Spelling
Poetry	Penmanship
Music	Art
Physical Education	

Don't forget that themes use a combination of fiction and non fiction in examining a topic's many dimensions, so have access to a large quantity of theme-related books and materials for your students to explore.

#3 Insert a Variety of Activities and Resources

Resources might include:

Books	Songs/Chants	Community Paper
Computer Programs	Dances	Field Trips
Games	Guest Speakers	Library
Magazines	Movies	Newspapers
Photo File	Poetry	Reference Material

Keep in mind that not every theme topic will utilize all these resources.

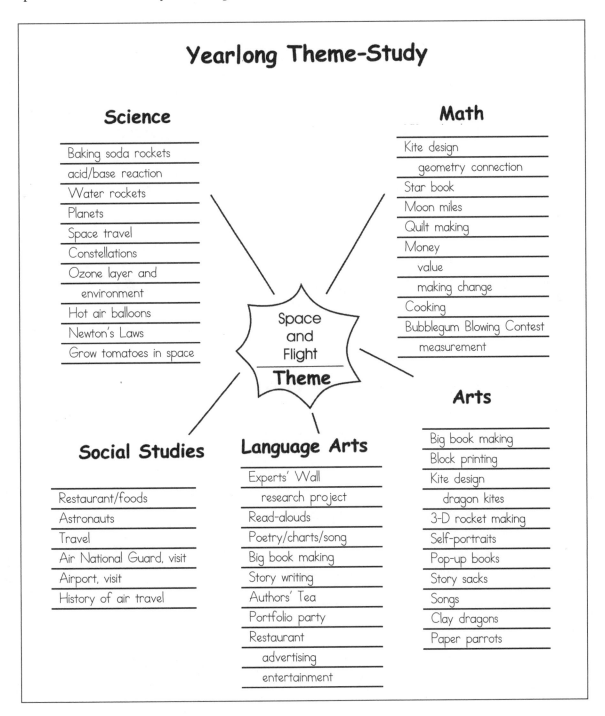

Theme-Study

Science

_____
_____
_____
_____
_____
_____
_____
_____
_____

Math

_____
_____
_____
_____
_____
_____
_____
_____
_____

Social Studies

_____
_____
_____
_____
_____
_____
_____

Theme

_____

Arts

_____
_____
_____
_____
_____
_____

Language Arts

_____
_____
_____
_____
_____
_____
_____
_____
_____

Reproducible

#4 Use Your Web to Lead Your Planning

Most topics will invite some linear investigations, but the nice thing about a web is that there is no clear beginning or ending—you can decide the order as you start teaching from it. Your web can help you show connections between your subject areas, thereby strengthening the learning for your students.

#5 Students Develop Webs Themselves

This technique works well for student-generated research topics and as a means to help organize story writing for the young child.

Question & Answer

How long should a theme last?

Some teachers plan several four-to-six-week themes, which by the end of the year will have covered and incorporated their entire curriculum. I use one yearlong theme-study, centered around a science or social studies unit, and incorporate several shorter subthemes (mini-units), each of which is connected to the larger theme. You may want to use a combination approach of shorter and longer theme-study units. Take your cue from your students and the subject matter. If students are excited about the theme you're studying and your instructional methods, consider working with the same theme all year. If your class moans every time you mention the theme-study, however, you might want to change it and rethink your approach to studying the new theme.

Space and Flight: A Yearlong Theme-Study

The remainder of this chapter will explore the use of theme-studies in the classroom through an in-depth look at a Room 6 yearlong unit on space and flight. Teachers can use several of the activity ideas I used in this study of space and flight—a theme kick-off activity, class-run restaurant, field trips, story sacks, book/video bags, etc.—with any theme-study. In fact, that is the beauty of teaching through themes. With a little adjustment, you can reuse good ideas and feel just as excited about them as you did the first time you tried them in the classroom. It is no longer "the same old thing," because the theme is different, and each year it brings a whole new level of interest, enjoyment, and anticipation! Sample work and reproducibles, applicable to any theme-study, are included throughout.

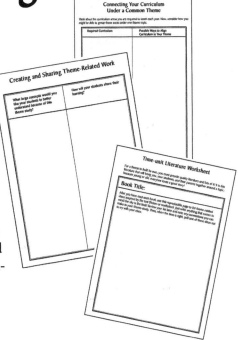

A Peek Inside Room 6

IN-DEPTH THEME-STUDY

Summer: Brainstorm, List, and Collect!

I began my investigation of this theme by listing all the possible topics (kites, airplanes, birds, rockets, space travel, the solar system, circus aerialists!) we could explore during the coming year. I knew that researching space and flight would be an enormous project, especially when you consider everything that flies, but in order to include all the science and social studies curriculum areas in our yearlong study, an expansive theme was exactly what I wanted.

During beginning of the the summer I gathered information and materials. I let my mind wander and my ideas flow—anything and everything is a possibility at this "messy" point in the planning process. Later in the summer I brought all my ideas together into more cohesive units of study, and as ideas jelled, I began to use some of my own theme planning form (see page 140).

As I compiled my initial ideas, I began to realize all the wonderful possibilities for our upcoming investigation—subthemes and mini-units about the atmosphere and gravitational pull would strengthen our science-based conversations, and I knew my own attendance at Space Camp in Huntsville, Alabama, would make for great related stories.

The possibilities abounded for reading, writing, math, science, social studies, and art projects, but the first thing I knew I needed to do was to gather literature—and lots of it! Needless to say, I found numerous books on the subject of space and flight.

Literature is a vital part of any theme-study, because it is the story element that will keep students involved with the main topic. Incorporate theme information right into your read-aloud sessions. (I recommend novel-length read-alouds.)

Summer Letter. I introduce the year's theme to students during the summer. This letter includes the highlights I am planning for the new school year, allowing students and parents to discuss the topic, formulate questions, and gather related artifacts. And I always let families know that their input is welcomed and needed. There is always room for change and adjustment.

Dear Room 6 Parents and Children:

With the summer just about over and school around the corner, I want to update you on the plans for this upcoming school year.

Our yearlong theme will revolve around space and flight. My husband, Jim, affectionately known as King "J" in Room 6, and I have been collecting books, videos, and artifacts on space and space exploration.

The art components in this yearlong theme will be dazzling—everything from a classroom quilt to big books, 3-D rocket making to Story Sacks! We will investigate the solar system and constellations. Did you know that the ancient Mayas built their cities and temples in perfect alliance with the night sky? These are some of the topics we'll be exploring.

The School Year: Ready, Set, . . . Fly!

Each year I brainstorm a fun activity to kick off our theme-study. By participating in such an event we not only learn about the project and all it entails, but we also learn about each other. The class is so engaged in the activity that we are open to working and sharing with one another, helping us to grow into a caring community of learners.

Kick-off Theme Activity: Kites

One of the "space and flight" items on my summer brainstorming lists was kites . . . all different kinds of kites! Their form is intriguing, and I discovered so many different varieties—from the simple dime-store kite to kites that had to be steered with two handles. I then looked for books on this subject matter, and I discovered some wonderful titles: *The Kite Flier*, by Dennis Haseley (Simon and Schuster), *The Sea Breeze Hotel*, by Marcia Vaughn and Peter Mullins (Harper Collins Children's Books), and *Dragon Kite of the Autumn Moon*, by Valerie Reddix (Lothrop, Lee, and Shepard Books). I also found the book *Making Kites*, by David Michael (Larousse Kingfisher Chambers), which became the source for one of our kick-off theme activities.

The Math, Science, and Art Connection. As we started discussing kites and studying their forms, Room 6 students came to the conclusion that the physical properties of kites directly correlates with their ability to fly, and immediately I knew a powerful math lesson was in the making! And when our art teacher found out what we were studying, she decided to address some of her curriculum instruction, such as line designs and patterns, that were also part of our math curriculum!

To test our kite-flying hypothesis, each student constructed his/her own kite using one of the basic forms found in David Michael's book. The children loved this art/science/math/cultural exploration, and the kites they produced were magnificent.

Community Builder. When the entire class had finished their kite construction, each student drew a picture of him/herself with his/her kite either in the air or on the ground. We then invited parents and other community members to join in our fun as we gave our kites a test fly. So on one beautiful day we tied strings on our kites and proceeded outside for an afternoon of fun and discovery! The students were thrilled! Teachers and parents aided struggling first-time kite flyers and, me included, tested a few kites out for ourselves. Admittedly, our success rate for our classroom-designed kites was low—most did not fly—but with the addition of the store-bought kites, we were still a high-flying crowd.

Although most of our kites didn't leave the ground, this activity had accomplished exactly what I had wanted it to—it brought the theme choice to life, energized everyone, and helped build community within our class!

A Peek
Inside
Room
6

IN-DEPTH
THEME-
STUDY

A Chance for Exploration. As we read more about kites we began to realize the cultural implications of kite flying (e.g., dragon kites of the orient and kite flying in Japan on Children's Day). We learned that in Japan kite fliers actually release their kites in order to carry away their miseries. From this discussion came a whole new mini-unit—the concept of dragons as mystical creatures that fly. We read stories and poems about dragons. We constructed dragons out of Lego's and Goo Goo Plex building materials. I found dragon poems to reproduce on charts, which the students read, acted out, and even sang to other classrooms. Eventually, our dragon-study turned to an excursion into fairy tales as a type of literature, and we read and compared fairy tales from different cultures.

Instructional Value. These charts also became the basis for much of my skill instruction in phonics and word analysis. We read and reread the poems in order to build fluency. The students loved every minute of it! We even constructed folded-paper dragon puppets to use in the classroom for impromptu puppet shows. The dragon mini-unit was beginning to fuel our imaginations and our interest in all things that fly.

Back on Earth: Theme-Related Activities

Eventually, our conversation turned to more conventional methods of flying here on earth. As luck would have it, the entire school's science program that year centered around birds of prey, which fit perfectly into our theme. We studied the characteristics of these birds—their feathers, beaks, feet—in great detail. We learned about different types of birds of prey. We even spent time dissecting owl pellets (a great activity for illustrating the natural food chain), and we were all surprised at the various bits and pieces of other animals we found in this refuse.

As the year progressed our study turned to air travel, space travel, the solar system, and constellations, and we made it a point to go to as many airports and planetariums as we could find in Vermont. Our first trip was to the Air National Guard, where they taught us about fighting planes and the jobs that pilots perform. A second trip, this time to Burlington International Airport, revealed the numerous careers associated with air travel. We visited the control tower and even spent time with the employees in the airport restaurant. The class had decided to try their hand at running a restaurant (open to the public) in order to raise money for our three-day class campout and field trip to the Christa McAuliffe Planetarium in Concord, New Hampshire. Our airport restaurant visit gave us insight into what we would need to do to start planning our new venture.

Keep in mind that while we used these activities in conjunction with our space-flight theme-study, you and your class can apply them to any theme or curriculum unit.

Restaurant Fundraiser

Have you ever thought of running a classroom restaurant? Well, with some helpful parents, eager students, and imagination, you and your class can create a theme-related fundraiser that accomplishes much more than just raising money! Here are the steps I followed when planning for the opening of Simmering Supernova Café.

1. Because running a restaurant is no small feat, the first thing you should do is secure parental support and assistance. Write a letter to parents that describes your idea and its benefits. Ask for volunteers who might be interested in forming the restaurant management team.

2. Once your management team is in place, discuss logistics with team members. You might also choose to discuss some of these details with students, too. Questions might include:

- Who will cook?
- Where will the cooking take place?
- How will students assist with cooking?
- How many weeks will you keep the restaurant open?
- How many days a week will students serve meals?
- At what time of day will students serve meals (e.g., breakfast, lunch, or dinner)?
- What are some of the different tasks students will have?
- Will your class need grant money or food donations to run the restaurant?
- What are the benefits for organizing such a task (reading, writing, math, social studies, art, and health connections; teaching responsibility and organization, etc.)?

3. With your class:

- Create a theme-related menu (see page 147 for sample menu).
- Set one price (per person) for each meal, or price items individually.
- Brainstorm a supplies list (e.g., napkins, plates, silverware, tables, chairs, tablecloths—bought, borrowed, or classroom set).
- Brainstorm a list of student roles and responsibilities, and discuss each:
  Do students want to provide entertainment while patrons are dining? If so, what type of entertainment?
- Who will serve as the waitstaff for the first week? the second? third?
- How should the restaurant be decorated?
- Divide students into "task teams."
- Contact local newspapers and radio stations and ask if they would be interested in publicizing the restaurant. Have students create advertisement posters to hang around town.
- Start organizing your restaurant!

Students Prepare Festive Theme-Related Foods! Room 6 students ran Simmering Supernova Café, our first classroom-run restaurant, for four meals, one meal per week, and we chose to serve each meal in our classroom during our school lunch hour. The first year we designed our menu around foods parents felt comfortable cooking. In the following years, however, the meals took on more exciting and exotic flavors as recipes complemented our classroom theme (see page 146 for sample menu from the Café).

A Peek Inside Room 6

IN-DEPTH THEME-STUDY

Students helped cook all the food we served (and we served a lot!). We prepared some of the food in the classroom, but students prepared the main dishes and desserts at one of the management team member's homes before the restaurant opened that day. (The food and workers often were arriving at the back door as the guests were arriving at the front door!)

For each meal the class designed and self-published a recipe book, complete with theme-related research, which they sold at each restaurant opening.

Wednesday, April 7, 1999 12:45 PM
Featuring the story of the Musicians of the Sun as performed by the students of Room 6, a game of Ancient American Jeopardy, and new and different tales each week.

Spicy Coffee, Cocoa, & Juices
Soup: Cheese
Bread: Corn Tortillas
Salsas (Verde & Roja) with chips & Quesadillas
Stuffed Chiles with Walnut Sauce or
Chicken & Cheese Flautas
Spicy Roasted Pumpkin
Mexican Rice
Cantaloupe Tart and Rice Pudding
Sopaipillas with sugar & honey
Spicy Coffee, Cocoa, & Juices
Soup: Tortilla

Friday, April 9, 1999 6:30 PM
Featuring the story of the Musicians of the Sun as performed by the students of Room 6, a game of Ancient American Jeopardy, and new and different tales each week.

Bread: Corn Tortillas
Salsas (Verde & Roja) with chips & Quesadillas
Chicken Tamales with Green Sauce
Roasted Corn with Red Salsa
Spicy Roasted Pumpkin
Mexican Rice
Cantaloupe Tart and Rice Pudding
Sopaipillas with sugar & honey
Spicy Coffee, Cocoa, & Juices
Soup: Tortilla

This particular menu was created for a different theme-study—Ancient Civilizations of the Americas. Because Simmering Supernova Café was our first classroom-run restaurant, we decided to create foods with which everyone was familiar. As you can see in the above menu, however, later recipes directly reflected the theme-study.

IN-DEPTH THEME-STUDY

Restaurant Responsibilities. Together, the entire class worked on theme-related classroom displays, and I wanted to have students experience all the different roles and responsibilities a restaurant has to offer, so I divided them into four groups. One group was in charge of the actual running of the restaurant—welcoming patrons, taking orders, waiting tables, etc.—per week. The other three groups were in charge of theme-related entertainment—dancing, singing, reading class—written poems, playing musical instruments, acting in plays, and even challenging guests to a game of theme-related jeopardy! Group responsibilities rotated each week.

Customer Satisfaction. At the conclusion of each meal we asked patrons to fill out a "Customer Comment Card," which directed them to rate the service, the food, and their overall experience. We also asked for written responses on what pieces of artwork they liked best and why, and what facts they learned from visiting the restaurant.

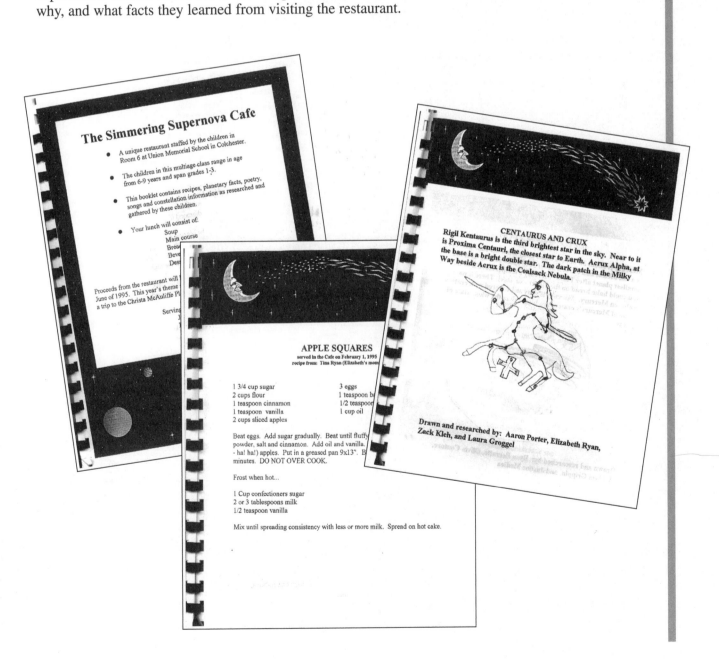

A Peek Inside Room 6

IN-DEPTH THEME-STUDY

RAJ CHAWLA, for the Free Press

Union class serves up edible lesson to public

By Jim Daley
Free Press Correspondent

COLCHESTER — Colchester's newest lunch-only restaurant, the Simmering Supernova Cafe, seated a diversified clientele in a packed room this week at Union Memorial School.

Students of Room 6 prepared the second of four noontime culinary adventures Wednesday.

The culinary project was organized by Union Memorial teacher Ellen Thompson as a way to teach 24 6- to 9-year-old students about the tasks involved in setting up, cooking and staffing a classroom restaurant.

Wednesday, host-cashier Max O'Hara-Shea, 7, expertly led WIZN radio personality Steve Cormier and his party to their table, where they were served by third-graders Drew Bahrenburg and Kristine Hamel.

Soon after, Navy helicopter pilot Brian Gebo, on leave from Jacksonville, Fla., Naval Air Station, his wife, Heather, and father, Jim Holzschuh of Alburg,

How about some lunch?

■ **What:** Lunch at the Simmering Supernova Cafe
■ **When:** 12:15 p.m. Wednesday and Feb. 15
■ **Where:** Union Memorial School, Room 6
■ **For reservations:** Call 878-1127
■ **Cost:** $4.50 per person

were served the soup course, a steaming bowl of minestrone, by first-graders Elizabeth Ryan and Kyle Weed.

Forty-one other diners, 16 more than expected, also enjoyed the calzone entree, an Italian turnover stuffed with ham, salami, spinach and at least three kinds of cheese. Breads, salads and apple squares for dessert tempted those with heartier appetites.

"Our school kitchen is used for the students' lunches," Thompson said, "so the kids prepared the basics here and, our chef, Tina Ryan, did the cooking

at home and brought the food back here." Ryan, who lives on Middle Road, is a former delicatessen and bakery chef for a Massachusetts grocery chain.

Thompson said support for the restaurant had come from throughout the town.

"Town office workers, library folks, local clergy, school board people have signed up, . . . and we even had nine take-out orders for a luncheon meeting at the school district office," she said.

And, as a side course, the students have learned something about radio broadcasting.

Cormier said several students went to the radio station, prepared, wrote and aired several public service announcements promoting the event.

Any profits the class earns will be used for a three-day student-parent campout and visit to the New Hampshire planetarium named for Christa McAuliffe, the teacher-astronaut who was killed Jan. 28, 1986, when the space shuttle Challenger exploded over the Atlantic Ocean.

Burlington Free Press 2/3/95

Reprinted with permission from: The Burlington Free Press, Burlington , VT.

Question & Answer

Why did you hold the restaurant in your classroom during the day?

We set the restaurant in the classroom during the day for several reasons, the most important of which was so that those community members who attended experienced the energy and learning of a busy, crowded public school—a time and place to see teaching and learning in action.

Operating the restaurant from the classroom allowed students to work in a familiar environment, one that displayed all our theme-related work.

IN-DEPTH THEME-STUDY

Artist-in-Residency

A wonderful addition to any classroom (theme-study or no) is an artist-in-residency. Some school districts/schools sponsor art-related programs in which artists of various disciplines visit individual schools. If, however, your school district/school does not support such a program, consider hosting your own artist-in-residency. (In years past I have written and received money from grants for such a program.) If you teach with theme-studies, look for one or more artists whose work somehow supports your theme to visit your classroom. If possible, plan evening events so parents can partake in this creative learning experience.

Story Sacks: Story Telling . . . Kid Style!

A story sack is a paper bag that students decorate and fill with artifacts—pictures, props, etc.—from a story they have just read. A story sack helps students tell about their stories without reading the entire book to others.

Once each year, Room 6 students make story sacks. They create these sacks in response to a book they have read themselves or one they have had read to them. Story sacks are easy to make, they allow for teachers to integrate science and social studies curriculum with language arts, and they are a powerful teaching tool. Use story sacks to teach and reinforce

- reading, listening comprehension, and oral presentation skills
- what a main idea is and what supporting textual details are
- cooperative group collaboration

Here's how to organize and manage this activity:

1. **Group** students into literature circles. These groups will work together on their book selection and the making of their story sack. I do not group students according to ability. I group them according to which students—of all ability levels—work well together.

2. **Gather** up all of your theme-related story books and hold a "book-talk" with your class. Select these books carefully—they should be so irresistible and interesting that students will be eager and excited to share them with the rest of the class. Discuss your theme-related picture books and the fact that some may be too difficult for students to read by themselves, some may be too easy, and some may be just right. You need and want all levels at this time.

3. **Share** the task with your students. Each student should be looking for a story that is so good they feel they can "tell" it without the book. At this point they start working on their story sack, putting in artifacts that will help them tell their chosen story to others. When the sack is finished students will share their stories with the school's kindergarten classes.

A Peek Inside Room 6

IN-DEPTH THEME-STUDY

4. **Select a story**. Each literature circle works together to share as many stories with each other as possible. Often students will read to one another, or a group will "hire" an adult to read aloud to them. The object for the group is to know as many stories as they can so they pick the best story—the one they want to share the most—to retell.

5. **Fill out a planning sheet**. Students fill out a story sack planning sheet (see page 151). They should discuss what materials they will need and what items they will want to put in their sacks.

6. **Create story sacks**. The groups work on their own sacks, collecting and creating items to support them in their retelling of the story to another person. Often students will want to decorate their sacks with the title of their story and a scene or two.

7. **Practice.** Students practice their story retellings using their story sacks.

8. **Storytelling.** When confident, students sign up to be a guest storyteller in a kindergarten classroom.

9. **Share with the community**. Students share these stories with their parents and family members at an "evening celebration of learning."

Name _____ Date _____

Story Sack Planning Sheet

Title of my book:

_____

_____

Materials I will need:

_____

_____

_____

_____

I plan to make:

_____

_____

_____

_____

A Peek Inside Room 6

IN-DEPTH THEME-STUDY

Traveling Book/Video Bag

The Traveling Book/Video Bag is a simple but powerful teaching tool that gives families the opportunity to learn more about the classroom theme-study. To assemble this bag, here's what you do:

- Find a cloth bag (the kind you receive at teacher conferences) that's in good condition.

- Choose a theme-related book or video (one that is sure to engage the entire family!) and place it in the bag. Also place in the bag a journal in which children and their parents can comment on the book/video—what they each liked about it, how it made them feel, etc. For me, the journal has been the most inspiring component of this activity as it allows students and parents to discuss their reaction to the book/video. Once the book starts traveling among classroom families, parents and students have the opportunity to read their peers' comments.

- In your summer letter to parents and students, explain the purpose of the Traveling Book/Video Bag. (See page 153 for letter reproducible.) Since the book is theme-related, it is my hope that students and their parents will start discussing our upcoming theme before the school year has even started.

- Send the bag home with one student. When s/he returns the bag, ask him/her to share his/her response and his/her family's response to the book or video.

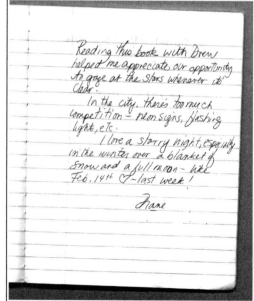

Traveling Book/Video Bag

Dear _____:

    Throughout the year your child will be selected to take home a Traveling Book/Video Bag to share at home with your family. This bag contains a book and/or video that complements our classroom theme.

When the book/video bag arrives at your house, here's what to do:
- Find a warm, cozy spot to read the book or watch the video together.

- Read the book aloud and discuss the story.

- Write in the Traveling Book/Video Journal, which you will find in the bag. You will notice that this is a blank journal. Your child should write a message, and, of course, you can add a message, too. Write and/or draw about your favorite part: What made you laugh? What made you think? What pictures did you like best, and why?

- Next, put the book and its journal back in the bag and have your child return it to school the next day. I will set aside in-class time during the next school day for your child to share with the class your family's written response.

    The book will soon travel once again, but this time to another child and his/her family. Thus, it is indeed a Traveling Book/Video Bag!

    As you can see, it will take a number of weeks before everyone gets to bring the book/video home. When this book/video completes the circuit, we will choose another book to travel. Enjoy!

A Peek Inside Room 6

IN-DEPTH THEME-STUDY

Moon Miles

The letter below talks aboout a fun family activity, Moon Miles.

January 3, 1995

Dear Parents:

Today we are beginning a new space-fitness project in Room 6. Please help your child participate by reading the directions below. You and your entire family are invited to participate, too!

Directions for Students:

1. Go for a walk. Better yet, go for a walk with someone in your family. Even better, go for a walk with someone in your family and your dog!

2. Keep track of the miles or partial miles you walked.

3. In class the next day record your mileage on the Moon Miles Recording Sheet. If you walked a mile, write 1. If you walked a mile with your dad, write 2 (1 mile for you, 1 mile for him). If you walked a mile with your dad and your dog, write 3. Get it? Everybody counts!

4. Bring the Moon Miles Recording Sheet to school after every walk. Bring home a new one to fill out.

5. At school the "Moon Miles Recorders" will add your mileage to the class chart.

Our goal is to walk the distance (in miles) between planet earth and the moon—239,900 miles, give or take a few! Now, relax. Each of our earth miles will equal 100 miles in space travel.

So, the challenge is on: We need to walk 2,399 miles before the campout! Help us, please!

Sincerely,

Ellen

Ellen Thompson (Ms. T.)

P.S. We have already enlisted all the specialist teachers who work with our class to help us out on this project.

The challenge begins . . . now!

A Peek
Inside
Room
6

IN-DEPTH
THEME-
STUDY

Campout

Planning for a class campout is not nearly as much work as you might think. The first step is to decide what destination would best support your classroom theme. Once the location is found, the rest, with some help and organization, falls into place.

I suggest you make this venture into a family outing. Enlisting the aid of parents accomplishes four very important goals:

- First, involving parents in their children's class-related learning allows students to share their knowledge and work with their parents firsthand.
- Second, seeking parents' assistance in organizing such a trip allows them to make their child's learning their learning, too. You are giving them ownership of an important segment of their child's education.
- Third, sharing responsibilities with others will allow you, the teacher, the opportunity take care of logistics but also enjoy the weekend with your students.
- And last but not least, the learning and interaction that takes place during a classroom campout helps make the learning real and the weekend a community-building experience to remember!

The letter to parents about our space and flight campout best explains this fun and informative classroom experience.

A Room 6 community-building experience.

Dear Parents:

Yes, it is true! Room 6 students earned almost $900.00 at Simmering Supernova Café, which is more than enough for us all to start planning for the annual Room 6 campout!

The campout is scheduled for the second weekend in June. We will leave Union Memorial School early Friday morning and will return Sunday afternoon. (I will be in touch with exact times.) Our destination is Bear Brook State Park, located just outside Concord, New Hampshire. We will plan to stop on our way at the Christa McAuliffe Planetarium, which we have reserved just for us! Cost for each student is . . . nothing!, thanks to the Simmering Supernova Café fundraiser. However, this is the only weekend in which extra money will go toward offsetting the costs for families who come along, as the available dates cannot be negotiated at this time.

Everyone—students and their families—is invited to attend this wonderful field trip! Of course, Room 6 students may attend the campout without a family member, but parents and siblings are strongly encouraged to participate. Believe me, you won't want to miss the fun!

Because this is a school field trip, there are outings and events planned during the weekend that all Room 6 students are required to attend—the planetarium trip, the annual lobster feed, and the compulsory "ghost stories around the campfire."

We Need Your Help! Let's make this a fun, student-centered weekend your children will never forget! Start thinking about a hobby or game you would like to share. We can plan for everything from tissue paper hot air balloon launches to necklace making to rocket launching to a rowdy game or two of softball!

But first, in order to get the campout up and running, we need helpers. Tina has volunteered to spearhead our food needs (Thanks, Tina!), but she needs volunteers to assist with organizing our meals and soliciting food donations from various Colchester businesses. This is a mighty job, so any help you can give Tina would be greatly appreciated.

We also need an activity organizer and a team of parents willing to supervise and participate in fun events for our "free" time at the campground. Campout "minstrels" (and our trip wouldn't be complete without them), it's time to practice your routines. I can think of a few people who would make perfect entertainers!

Think about the weekend and fill out the attached sign-up as soon as possible. I will plan to have a campout meeting one evening later in the spring as we approach this exciting event.

Thanks for your help!

Ellen

Ellen Thompson (Ms. T.)

Sample Campout Letter

Campout Permission Form

Name _____

How many people will be camping with you? (estimated number) _____

Will you be camping in a pop-up, a self-contained RV, or a tent? (please circle the correct choice)

Would you consider signing up for any of the following?

✔ Food Director (Tina)

___ Activities Director

___ Entertainment Director (Lead Minstrel)

___ Food Committee

___ Activities Team

___ Entertainment Committee

___ Other: _____

I have an idea to share:

_____

Please return this to school by Wednesday, March 11, at the latest, as we cannot reserve a campground without this information. If you are not exact at this time, don't fret—I just need to have a rough estimate of how many people plan to attend and what they plan to camp out in. Thanks!

IN-DEPTH THEME-STUDY

Authors' Tea: What a Celebration!

The Authors' Tea is an annual culminating activity planned to celebrate the entire year of writing in Room 6. It is a celebration for students, families, and me.

An Authors' Tea is easy to plan, and it can complement any theme-study you are teaching. I usually plan it as an evening event during the month of May, but you may decide to host it during the day at any point within the school year; it depends on the space you have available and the time(s) that will work best for your students and their parents.

Two Weeks Before the Tea. Two weeks before the authors' celebration have students choose one piece of writing they have worked on during the year they would like to read the evening of the Tea, and set aside classroom time for students to practice reading their pieces. I have found that authors are usually very selective about the writing they choose because they know they are going to read it before an audience. After students have chosen their piece, I create a program for the audience based on their selections.

The Evening of the Tea. Once students and families arrive they take a seat in the school's multipurpose room, where we have traditionally held this performance. After everyone has found a place to sit, it is time for one of the students (a volunteer master of ceremonies) to welcome family and friends and introduce the first four authors. (Before families arrive I place four stools up on the stage. I also try to have a microphone available for students to use during their reading.)

Each student begins his/her reading by introducing him/herself and sharing the titles of all the books s/he has written throughout the year. Wild applause explodes from parents and siblings at the conclusion of each piece, and after one group of four has finished its readings and students have taken a seat next to their families in the audience, a second group of four takes the stage. This continues until each author has read. A selected student (again, a volunteer) will then close out the ceremony by inviting everyone to partake in the "literary snacks"— which can be anything from Alphabets cereal snack mix to Frobscottle—brought in by the families. (Frobscottle, by the way, is the favorite drink of the Big Friendly Giant in Roald

Authors' Tea Celebration! We usually hold this event in our school's multipurpose room, but this particular year we held it right in Room 6!

Question & Answer

What elements make up a "good" story?

In Room 6 we use the Vermont Writing Rubric to help us determine what qualifies as "good" writing.

Characteristics for a good story include the following:
- Does the story have a purpose?
- Is the story well organized?
- Do the details support and strengthen the story?
- Is the voice consistent throughout the story? Is the tone consistent?
- Is the appropriate grammar, punctuation, and spelling used?
- Throughout the writing process, of course, I discuss these terms and elements with students.

A Peek Inside Room 6

IN-DEPTH THEME-STUDY

Dahl's book, *The Big Friendly Giant*.)

Experts' Wall

Experts' Wall can be a very powerful component to any theme-study. As students talk and read about the classroom theme, they usually ask a multitude of questions. In order to capture and respond to these questions, here's what to do:

1. Write questions on strips of paper as students ask them and attach them to your "Experts' Wall," a designated area (bulletin board, wall space) in the classroom.

2. Toward the middle of the theme, when the wall is filled, take questions down. Teach students how to research for the answers. Have students form groups based around their question choices.

3. To assist students in their research, use a simple recording system, a fact collection sheet on which students document information, from at least three sources, about their question. Each strip holds one fact. Show students how to designate a different number for each source. The numbers indicate from what source the information originated.

4. Have students cut apart their fact strips and show them how to classify facts into groups according to each strip's content focus. Next, have students begin writing their reports and/or creating the responses they will eventually share with the class and their parents.

5. Once they have sorted their facts and read each fact-group over, students should place that group out of reach and write, in their own words, a paragraph using the information from that pile. Students should repeat this procedure until they have read through all their fact-piles. (This segment of the project creates the body of their researched response.)

This exercise helps students avoid "copying out of the book" syndrome, since they know where their information comes from.

A Peek Inside Room 6

IN-DEPTH THEME-STUDY

6. Instruct students about how to write opening and closing paragraphs (talk with them about the terms opening/introduction, body text, closing/conclusion).

7. Once the research is complete, students can create posters or reports to showcase this new information for others, or hold an "Experts' Wall Extravaganza," an evening where students can share information with their families and with one another.

Experts' Wall Fact Collection Sheet

Source # 1

Title: To Space and Back

Author(s): Sally Ride with Susan Okie

City and state where published: New York, NY   **Publisher:** Lothrop, Lee & Shepard Books

Year published: 1986   **ISBN #:** 0-688-06159-1

Read through your book, magazine, newspaper article, video, or computer program. Look for interesting facts on your topic area. Write one fact in each box below. Use a different number for each source (book, magazine, video, etc.) Please note the number (#) ____ you have designated for that piece of information on each. You will have to check with your group to make sure you don't repeat a number.

- -

Source # 1   **Fact #** 1

The space shuttle is 30 feet high.

- -

Source # 1   **Fact #** 2

It stands on its tail on the launch pad.

- -

Source # 1   **Fact #** 3

The astronauts lie on their back when they take off.

- -

Source # 1   **Fact #** 4

The rockets burn out and drop off in two minutes from blastoff.

Experts' Wall Fact Collection Sheet

Source #

Title:

Author(s):

City and state where published:

Year published: **ISBN #:**

Read through your book, magazine, newspaper article, video, or computer program. Look for interesting facts on your topic area. Write one fact in each box below. Use a different number for each source (book, magazine, video, etc.) Please note the number (#) _____ you have designated for that piece of information on each. You will have to check with your group to make sure you don't repeat a number.

- -

Source #   Fact #

- -

Source #   Fact #

- -

Source #   Fact #

- -

Source #   Fact #

IN-DEPTH THEME-STUDY

Making Big Books

Making big books is a fun activity students can do at various times during the school year. Creating these big books helps strengthen reading, writing, and collaborative-work skills. Here's what to do:

- As a class, select a favorite read-aloud and recreate it in larger form, using various art techniques to illustrate the story.

- Study the author and illustrator's work, recreating illustrations as true to the story as possible.

- Divide students into pairs to illustrate a page from the read-aloud, one that requires them to read their text piece and illustrate its main idea.

Room 6 students created several stories based on already published stories, including the following:

- *Papa, Give Me the Moon*, by Eric Carle (Simon and Schuster Children's), features the different phases of the moon.

- *The Z Was Zapped*, by Chris Van Allsburg (Houghton Mifflin), is an alphabet book told in the form of one-act plays in which the reader guesses what each picture is trying to show before turning to the answer on the back of the page. Our own version of this book, "The A Was Attacked by Aliens!", included pictures created by student pairs and alliteration riddles for each letter. Our book was filled with facts about each planet.

- *Animalia*, by Graeme Base (Penguin USA), is another alphabet book, one in which the students and I created sentences and a variety of illustrations for each letter.

If the selected story doesn't fit your classroom theme exactly, replace some of the words in order to create something more closely related. Or try writing your own book with the class, using the form from the chosen text as a template after which to mirror your story. Students love to read these beautiful creations over and over again.

During our space and flight theme-study, for instance, we created an interactive story that combined space travel with proper nutrition.
To create this interactive book, here's what we did:

- I created a paper doll astronaut template that would fit on a 12"x18" piece of black construction paper. The astronaut's helmet served as a place where students could paste their school picture.

- Students "spatter-painted" the black construction paper pieces to make them look like they were covered with stars.

- Students traced, cut out, and decorated their astronaut before they pasted it on their piece of black construction paper.

- Once the astronaut was attached to the paper, we added the frame sentence: "Astronaut _____ eats _____." Each student had to write his/her last name in the blank space after the word "Astronaut."

- Next we discussed nutrition and brainstormed a variety of healthy, balanced lunches.

- I then attached lunch bags to each astronaut page, and the students selected, drew, and cut out various lunch foods. Once this was done, students labeled meal items with their proper names and the food group to which each item belonged.

• Students then selected a meal and placed the items for this meal into their astronaut's lunch page. In order for readers to view the meal items, they had to pull them out of each bag!

Making Big Books with Community Paper

Create your own textured papers rather than using regular colored construction paper by making community paper with your class. Community paper, a term coined by friend and art teacher Ann Joppe-Mercure, is shared by all members of the class for a special project. No one "owns" the paper. Everyone uses what they need.

Community paper makes our class books and projects more colorful, textured, vibrant, and durable than crayon or marker print. Make this paper right in the classroom by setting up various paper-creation stations.

Here's how to make different community papers. (*Note:* Supplies below can be purchased at most art supply stores.)

Bubble paint: In a small plastic container, mix tempera paint with water (ratio of 1:4) and one teaspoon of dishwashing liquid. Add a straw. Blow into the mixture until the bubbles come up over the edge of the container. Take a piece of drawing paper and "pop" the bubbles onto it. Overlap the pops and create a fun paper.

Tempera paint: Use two or more colors of tempera paint; cover entire surface of paper with various colors and textures, using a dry paintbrush, or place drops on the edge of the paper, smearing the paint with a piece of cardboard.

Spatter paint: Use a toothbrush with tempera cakes or tempera paint; push paint over the edge of a piece of cardboard or a spoon to create a spatter effect.

Tissue collage: Use diluted white glue and water; cover plain construction paper with torn tissue of various sizes and colors, and paint with glue mixture.

Texture rubbings: Cover texture (e.g., brick, comb, flower) with paper; rub with side of crayon.

Marbleized paper: Use inks/kits for making marbleized papers.

Monoprint: Paint table with finger paint, create texture, place clean paper on top, rub, lift.

Sponge printing: Use sponges of differing textures to print landscapes, seascapes, or other geography. After sponged paint has dried, add details with a fine-tip marker or colored pencil.

Wet into wet: Wet paper with water; drip in watercolors; add salt on wet and watercolor paper to produce a crystal-like effect.

Resist: Draw with crayon or oil pastels; paint over with watercolor wash.

Chalk: Cut paper stencil; put chalk on stencil; push chalk off stencil onto paper so the chalk colors in around the stencil but leaves the stencil shape white.

Colored water-colored pencil: Draw, paint over with water or dip in water, then draw again.

Dry and store these papers for future use!

IN-DEPTH THEME-STUDY

A Theme-Related Journal

For our space and flight theme each student created a "Sky Watch Journal/Scavenger Hunt." Because the basis for the journal/scavenger hunt is observation, you can apply this same idea to any theme-study.

We created our journals by covering paper with the bubble painting technique (see page 163) and sewing pages together with a three-hole stitch. Once completed, students took their journals home and observed the night sky several times each week. They recorded their observations with pictures and words.

At the end of each month students brought journals into school to compare and discuss everything they had seen.

Remember, you can use this template to create journals that go along with any theme-study.

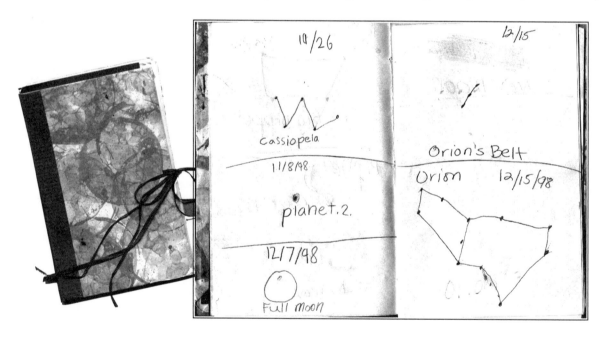

Sky Watch Scavenger Hunt

What can you find in your night sky? Look for these items and record your findings in this journal. You can draw and write about them. Be sure to label your drawings and date them. When you complete the scavenger hunt, bring your book to school.

Full moon	North Star	Milky Way
Half moon	Other	Meteors (falling stars)
Quarter moon	Orion's belt	
New moon	Other constellations	**Satellites**
Big Dipper	Planets	

**IN-DEPTH
THEME-
STUDY**

Directions for How to Make a Journal

1. To make cover paper: Cut two pieces of white construction paper into 6¼" x 10½" pieces. (You will eventually attach these two pieces with glue onto two pieces of cardboard, which will serve as the journal's front and back covers.)

2. To decorate cover paper: Use any one of the paper-painting techniques as described on page 163 to decorate both pieces of white construction paper.

3. To make cardboard cover base for front and back covers: Cut two pieces of cardboard into 4¼" x 8½ " pieces. (These two pieces will serve as the front and back of the journal.)

4. To cover exposed side of the cardboard covers: Lay one piece of the decorated paper, decorated side down, on a flat surface. Spread white glue until the cardboard is covered with a clear, thin layer of glue. Now, center and lay down one of the cardboard pieces on top of the undecorated side. Fold the excess decorated paper over the edge of the card-board onto the exposed side. Repeat with second set of paper and cardboard.

5. To create a journal spine: Cut a 10" strip of book tape (duct tape) and lay the nonsticky side down on a flat surface. Now, take the piece of decorated cardboard that will serve as your front cover and lay it flat on top of one half of the tape. Repeat with the back cover.

6. To create journal pages: Take any number of 8 ½"

Glue and fold over

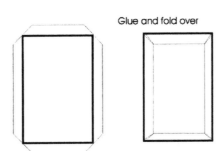

Fold down

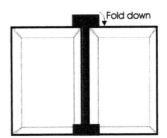

**IN-DEPTH
THEME-
STUDY**

x 11" pieces of white paper (you can decide how many pages the journal needs) and fold them in half (horizontally).

Take a piece of 8½" x 11" colored construction paper and also fold it in half (horizontally). Insert the folded journal pages into the folded construction paper.

Before you insert the pages into the front/back covers, punch three holes, evenly spaced, through the folded pages.

With a needle and dental floss, stitch the pages together.

Tie the two ends of dental floss together and cut off excess floss.

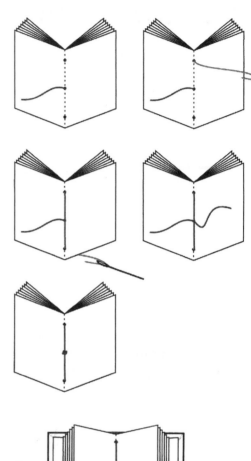

7. To insert tied pages into covers: Fold open the colored construction paper pages and glue one side to the inside of the front cover. Glue the other side to the inside of the back cover.

8. To keep journal from opening when not being used: Punch a hole on the outer edge of the front and back covers. Insert paper or satin ribbon through each and knot or tape. Keep journal closed by tying ribbons together.

Glue end papers inside cover

Quilt Making

Room 6 students usually create a quilt to illustrate part of the class theme-study. During our theme-study on space and flight, for example, Room 6 students created a fantasy quilt and submitted it to a contest being held at Disney World in Florida. Students designed fanciful flying objects using paper and fabric crayons, which were added to a large open panel in the center of the quilt and bordered with cloth. They then helped tie the quilt layers by hand after it was sewn together by a room mom. Our mini flying-world quilt was a runner up and was actually displayed at the park!

Now, don't panic . . . I do not sew! Fortunately, I have found crafty parents, fellow teachers, and local fabric store employees who are thrilled to help with such projects.

A Room 6 original! This fanciful classroom creation was a runner-up in a Disney World contest!

IN-DEPTH THEME-STUDY

Finger Puppets

Students love creating their own theme-related finger puppets! A great material to use when making these puppets is Model Magic, produced by Crayola. This white modeling compound, which feels a little like Styrofoam when dry, is easy to mold into shapes for finger puppets. Once it has dried, students can paint their puppets to make them look like a theme-related character or object.

Construction Paper Puppet

Materials and equipment:
  12"x18" construction paper
  Glue
  Construction paper scraps
  Scissors

Fold 12"x18" paper in thirds the long way

Fold in half

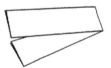

Fold back again

Staple inside to hold together

Decorate

  Fold tabs for 3-D effect

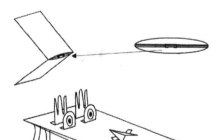

Reprinted with permission from Ann Joppe-Mercure

THE PARENT-COMMUNITY CONNECTION

You will discover that parents of first-grade students are usually more concerned about their child's academics than parents of children in other grades, because society has worked hard at making us all believe that this grade is the first *real* year of school. As teachers, we are much more aware of the realities of this age group, and thus it is our responsibility to allay apprehensions and clear up misconceptions parents might harbor. Verbal and written communications are, therefore, helpful and necessary tools.

Establish a regular communication schedule with your parent group from the very beginning of the school year. Most parents are curious and concerned about their child's progress in your classroom and want to feel included in the educational program. They want to better understand what their child is learning, and they want to know how they can help with this process. When parents are unsure of what is happening in your classroom, they are much less apt to volunteer for projects and are much more apt to discuss with other parents what they "think" is happening. Because this is inevitable, become part of the information cycle by planning your communication pieces, such as a summer "welcome letter," before the new school year begins.

Welcome Parents Into Your Classroom

Summer Welcome Letter

During the month of August, consider sending a welcome letter to your new class. This letter gives you the opportunity to introduce yourself and it allows you to answer some of your new parents' first questions before school begins (e.g., lunch program information, dress required for phys. ed., academic program, and theme-study, etc.). A welcome letter also allows you the opportunity to describe how parents can volunteer in the classroom. In the letter, enclose one or more fun activities for each child to complete, such as a family portrait (page 172) or student goal setting profile (page 174), for the first day of school. These activities will become the basis for some of your first group learning experiences.

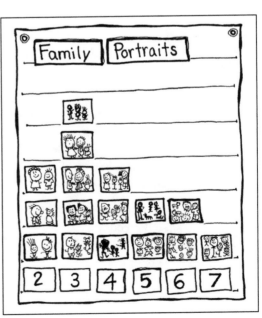

August 24

Dear Room 6 Parents and Children:

With the summer just about over and school around the corner, I want to update you on the plans for this upcoming school year.

Our year-long theme will revolve around ancient civilizations of the Americas. My husband, Jim (affectionately known as King "J" in Room 6) and I have been collecting books, videos, and artifacts on several civilizations, including the Mayas, Aztecs, Incas, and North American mound builders. And after a very exciting adventure while studying ancient Egypt last year, I know we will enjoy exploring the concept of pyramids and temples indicative of these cultures. We will also, of course, compare and contrast these complex civilizations.

The art components in this year-long theme will be dazzling—everything from weaving to pottery to cloth pictures to yarn pictures. We will compare weather patterns that occur in northern Vermont to those that occur in southern Mexico. Our data will be "crunched" on our classroom computers, giving the children insight as to how computers can help with this type of information. And, of course, we will use the Internet to find out the answers to our weather questions. We will also investigate the solar system and constellations! Did you know that the ancient Mayas built their cities and temples in perfect alliance with the night sky? These are some of the topics we'll be exploring.

The classroom has changed quite a bit over the summer, too, thanks once again to Jim. With the help of a PTO grant, Jim constructed an awesome loft, which the children will love. As most of you know, the only way to create space in Room 6 is to go up, so we did! Now Broccoli, our class iguana, will be at eye-level with all of the Room 6 "loft dwellers." The loft is carpeted, with the computer center located on the "first" floor. I see the "second" floor as the home for our classroom puppets. The railing can double as a perfect puppet stage! We're even thinking that the loft could be extra seating for our class-run restaurant...a mezzanine, if you will!

The Colchester School District is continuing in earnest its involvement with goal setting for students and families. In the earliest grades, there will be an emphasis on understanding the basic principles of the goal-setting process. Beginning in grade three, children will regularly set academic goals that support the Vermont Common Core. As many of you know, goal setting is not new to Room 6. For the past two years we have used this practice in both academic and behavioral progress. Students learn how to choose appropriate goals and achieve those goals with assistance from me or their classmates. This process helps Room 6 children better understand their growth as students. And it is such fun to witness a student achieve a goal for which they have had to work quite hard. We will document all their hard work in the "Traveling Goal Journals," just like last year.

We have been invited to be buddies with Mrs. Anderson's kindergarten class this year. This should be great fun for everyone. We are planning lots of reading time together, plus some intergenerational events. We hope to visit the Colchester Senior Center and maybe a center in South Burlington, too.

I have been busy this summer, traveling as usual. I spent a good share of June and July talking with teachers across the country. I visited teachers in Ohio, Oklahoma, New York, Maryland, Illinois, Michigan, and Wisconsin. As always, I shared details about our classroom and how we do "business" in Room 6.

Sample End-of-the-Summer Letter

The rest of the summer was spent playing with my big sister, Sally, who visited for several weeks. We swam in the lake and kayaked all over the outer bay. We peeked at ospreys in their nests and even had a pair keep close check on us as we paddled a little too close to their home. In addition, Jim and I helped our mothers move into new apartments in South Burlington. They are enjoying their new digs and are both getting used to life in this northern city. Jim's mom moved from Middlebury, Vermont, while my mom moved from Dedham, Massachusetts. I can't wait to see my mom's reaction to her first Vermont winter!

We will have a **Parents' Night** very early in the year. The date has been set for Wednesday, September 9, 1998, at 6:30 PM in Room 6. This will be a great evening for us to gather with ideas and questions about the year, and the "old fogey" parents will have lots of stories to share. This is a fun, informative evening, a wonderful chance to renew old friendships and begin new ones. Keep an eye out for more details shortly after school begins.

As you know, parent and community class volunteers are always welcome in Room 6! If you enjoy helping children in a particular curriculum area, working on activities such as the class newsletter, or reading with one or more students, this is the room for you! Please let me know if you have a particular and consistent time during the week that you could volunteer. We also welcome "drop-in" volunteers if you're weekly schedule varies. Also, if you have a particular skill (e.g., sewing, building, music, etc.) you would like to share with us, please let me know. We look forward to seeing you in Room 6!

I have enclosed some information for you to peek at before school starts on Tuesday, September 1st. YIKES! I am getting so excited to see you all again, and I can't wait to meet and get to know all of our new parents, too!

I will be in school every day this week. If you would like to stop in and visit, please do! I still like to sleep late (some things will never change), so look for me in Room 6 after 10:00 a.m. On Monday, August 31st, I will be at school from 2:00 p.m. on until . . . who knows!

See you soon;

Sincerely,

Ellen

Family Portrait

Name _____

Directions: Draw a picture of your family. Include any pets.

Family Portrait Follow-up Activity

Objectives for this activity include:

- Counting: one-to-one correspondence
- Community building: sharing about ourselves
- Basic bar graph information
- Math language: fewest, biggest, difference, same as, etc.
- Numeral sight-vocabulary matched with numeral formation

1. Ask each child to share his/her family picture. (For students who do not bring in a picture, set classroom time aside for them to draw one.)
2. Each student should then count their family members, including their pets. Have students share this number. Model by sharing your picture and the number of people in your family.
3. Create with students a graph out of everyone's family picture. I use a pocket chart (fabric backing with acetate pockets) which I label with the numbers represented in our pictures. I usually write out the number and include the digit.
4. Ask students to add their picture to the graph.

Now you have lots to talk about! Discuss which number represents the greatest number of people in a family and which number represents the fewest, and what the difference is between these numbers. This graph can help start lots of math-talk in your classroom.

Extension
1. Give each student a blank piece of paper.
2. Ask students to write the number of family members represented in their picture.
3. Ask students for suggestions about other ways they can make this number.
4. Model your number with Unifix cubes, find groups of objects that equal the number, and/or write combinations of numerals in equations. Record this information on a large sheet of paper for everyone to view. Now, ask the students to record the different ways they are able to represent their family number.

After everyone has completed this exercise, call the group back together to share their representations. Family pictures and their numerical representations can then be hung on the bulletin board. Such displays are great for open house! This also gives you an opportunity to meet families through each child's eyes.

Note: This activity helps you identify students who are strong in math and students who might struggle. For students who demonstrate aptitude, encourage them to experiment with subtraction and even multiplication. Let them try it all!

Student Goal-Setting Profile

Name: _____   Date: _____

Things I like...

Things I don't like...

ME

My favorite school activity...

This is what my family looks like...

Parents Night

Begin the school year with a night just for the parents and request that parents leave their children at home with a "kid" sitter. Because finding a sitter is sometimes difficult, and as some parents are financially burdened, talk with your PTO president about exploring other options such as in-school child care. On occasion, my son has even watched students in another classroom while evening meetings are taking place.

At your Parents Night:

- Share information about yourself, your teaching style, and what you hope to accomplish with students in the upcoming school year.
- Identify tasks with which parents can assist you (in-school helper or home volunteer work).
- Answer questions about homework and other responsibilities.
- Let parents know how to communicate with you if they are concerned, joyous, or just plain confused.

This one meeting has helped me more than letters or even phone calls (although phone calls are important, too). In person, the parents have a chance to better understand your classroom. A videotape of the class in action is a good way to start the evening presentation. This allows parents to see on screen what you have been describing in words. They will also now understand and recognize the words their child uses as s/he describes class routines. Together you will discover your goals are the same: you all want happy children who love to go to school and learn.

Parents night allows teachers to explain their educational program and upcoming events for the year.

Question & Answer

Is Parents Night the same as Open House?

No, Parents Night is an informational evening where parents come to find out particular information about the educational program, special events, and volunteer opportunities. I also write a follow-up letter to this meeting that I send to all parents. This is especially helpful to those parents who were not able to attend.

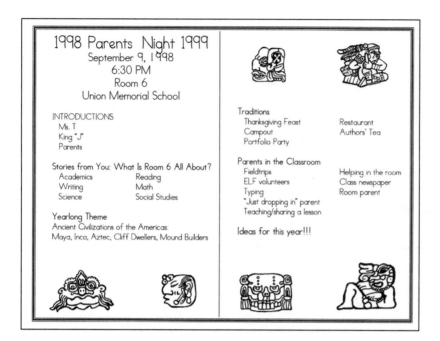

1998 Parents Night 1999
September 9, 1998
6:30 PM
Room 6
Union Memorial School

INTRODUCTIONS
Ms. T
King "J"
Parents

Stories from You: What Is Room 6 All About?
Academics   Reading
Writing   Math
Science   Social Studies

Yearlong Theme
Ancient Civilizations of the Americas:
Maya, Inca, Aztec, Cliff Dwellers, Mound Builders

Traditions
Thanksgiving Feast   Restaurant
Campout   Authors' Tea
Portfolio Party

Parents in the Classroom
Fieldtrips   Helping in the room
ELF volunteers   Class newspaper
Typing   Room parent
"Just dropping in" parent
Teaching/sharing a lesson

Ideas for this year!!!

Pictures correspond with our year-long theme. During this particular year we were studying ancient civilizations of the Americas.

Open House

Most schools offer an open house celebration for students and their parents. If your school does not host such an evening, consider holding one for your classroom. On this night the students are in charge, and they are excited about it! It is their night to share their school and classroom with their family. Open house evenings help reinforce the fact that we all need times to showcase our learning with others. It is a powerful evening of educational fun.

Many teachers brainstorm creative ways to engage family members in their classroom learning. For example, I have constructed a scavenger hunt (see page 177) for my students to complete with their families. I make up a list of people and places to visit on open house night. The use of a scavenger hunt or a question sheet ensures that parents will visit a variety of areas within the room and school.

After collecting these names, create a graph with your students to showcase information and illustrate mathematical properties. Graph topics might include: adults/children, male/female; number of brothers/sisters, etc. Discuss terms such as "graph," "fewer than," "greater than," and initiate all the possible counting opportunities.

"Eat-in-the-Room" Day

With your students, choose one day of the week to eat lunch in the room and have students invite their parents. (You can remind parents about this weekly event in your classroom newsletter.) It's simple, just bring food trays back from the cafeteria, pull chairs around different tables, play your favorite music, and chat. Students love this time with their parents and peers; parents enjoy it; and everyone gets a needed break from the busy school cafeteria.

Open House Scavenger Hunt

Name: _____

Directions:

1. Sign in.
2. On a separate sheet of paper write the names of the people who came to Open House with you.
   You will find this paper in the classroom. Put the names in the collection box. We will add each of the names to our class graph tomorrow morning.
3. Try to find and/or do each of the items on this sheet.

1. Introduce your family to your teacher.
2. Share a book that you have read in school.
3. Play your favorite math game.
4. See if your family can find your self-portrait on the wall.
5. Show your family where you keep your things in the classroom.
6. Introduce the class pets.
7. Introduce your family to a student in the classroom.
8. Show your family something on the computer.
9. Visit the other classrooms in the building:

library   gym   art room   music room   cafeteria

If the instructors are available, introduce your parents to them.

10. Say hello to the principal.

How Parents Can Help Their Children at Home

Reading at Home

Parents are constantly looking for learning-reinforcement activities they can do at home with their children. Often they request homework—drill-and-skill worksheets—but at the beginning of each school year I explain to these parents that other types of activities, such as reading with their child or overseeing their child's independent reading, will better support their daughter or son in school.

Although there are exceptions (see Homework Pockets, page 179), "drill-and-skill" homework usually requires very little thought, and because it isn't challenging, it quickly becomes boring and tedious. For most students, the only thing they accomplish by performing this task is the act of finishing their homework. Normally, such a goal is encouraged, but when students start doing their homework because it's easy to "get over with," assignments lose educational value. As such, I try very hard from the beginning of each school year to explain to parents the many other types of activities they can do to support their child in school. The assignments I share are meant to reinforce academic skills, set in motion good study habits, and demonstrate the joy new learning can bring.

Question & Answer

What type of homework do you assign to your students?

I encourage families to value real literacy events in their home, such as reading aloud, reading silently, watching educational television shows, writing stories on the computer, writing letters to family members and friends, and playing card games and board games in which students have to use math and problem-solving skills. For many parents, this might look like "fun" work, but stick with it and explain to them that learning should have an element of fun!

Homework Bags

One strategy to encourage parent-child at-home literacy activities is to create several homework bags. Since each bag contains a variety of activities, students can take the same bag home more than once. (Due to the number of bags and activities, each student takes home a bag an average of once a week).

In each bag include the following:
- a book students and parents can read aloud and/or a book-on-tape they can listen to
- three or four math games
- two or three language arts related games
- an empty journal into which parents and students can record their favorite choices. Students share their journal responses when they return their bag to school.
- instructions that direct students to choose and complete just three activities. (It usually takes them two or three days to return the bag with their activities.)

I assemble four or five bags. Activities usually remain the same during the year, so once I have finished my initial assembly, maintenance is very simple.

Homework Pockets

Sometimes "paper-and-pencil" (a.k.a., "drill-and-skill") homework activities such as reviewing and practicing penmanship consume valuable classroom time. By assigning students such activities to work on with their parents, you free additional instructional time for other classroom activities.

Here's how to create homework pockets for your students:
- Have each student decorate a manila folder, then laminate it so only the top is open and accessible.

- Place homework expectations for the entire week and a homework journal in the laminated folder. (See homework journal page below.)

- Starting in January, assign a specific day when folders are due back in class. (I usually hand folders out on a Tuesday and expect them back seven days later, on a Monday.) At fifteen minutes a night, the homework takes less than one week to complete. In Room 6 students do not need to complete all work by Monday, but they do have to bring the folders in nonetheless so I can review what they have/have not accomplished and read their feedback in the homework journal. This allows me to determine what and how much homework to give each student. It allows the assignment to remain manageable and successful.

Suggest to parents that they set aside fifteen to twenty minutes each night for homework. This encourages families to schedule homework time into their nightly routine. In addition, advise parents to limit the amount of time their son or daughter spends on home-school activities, as children at this age might become tired and frustrated with lengthy assignments.

Book Club: Home-School Reading Connection

Book Club has held an important place in my school-home folders for over fifteen years! Needless to say, this has been a successful exercise. Book Club works as follows:

- Along with activity directions, send a letter home to parents that explains Book Club. (See page 181 for sample letter.)

- Directions should advise parents to read aloud to their children for at least ten minutes every night. (Students can also read aloud to themselves or to a family member.) Students keep track of how many minutes parents read to them, and then bring this number into school.

- Students record their reading in increments of 100 minutes by placing a sticker on their individual reading chart. In Room 6 each student's chart corresponded to our theme-study. To create this or a similar chart, simply laminate a theme-related student-made drawing, magazine photograph, or illustration. For every 100 minutes, students place a sticker on their chart.

- For every 500 minutes (five stickers) spent reading, the student gets to choose one free book. (I have usually received the books I give students for free through my bonus points I have collected from various monthly book clubs. These book club newsletters also alert me to books I can buy at a discount.)

- Send home a list of students' favorite books. Your list might include:

    - *Superfudge*, Judy Blume (Bantam Doubleday Dell Books for Young Readers)
    - *Sarah, Plain and Tall*, Patricia MacLachlan (HarperCollins Children's Books)
    - *How to Eat Fried Worms*, Thomas Rockwell (Bantam Doubleday Books for Young Readers)
    - *The Not Just Anybody Family*, Shel Silverstein (HarperCollins Children's Books)
    - *A Light in the Attic*, Shel Silverstein (HarperCollins Children's Books)
    - *Falling Up: Poems and Drawings*, Shel Silverstein (HarperCollins Children's Books)

I often choose lengthier books because it forces a family to read a book over time. Inevitably, everyone in the family wants to hear what happens, what adventure the next chapter brings. Like me, you will love hearing from students just how special Book Club time is. After all, reading should be a pleasant experience modeled by the people we love. It is this type of interaction that will help reading become a lifelong habit for your students.

Traveling Book/Video Bag

The Traveling Book/Video Bag contains a book or video—one that complements your classroom theme—for students to share with their families. (See page 152, for more information on the Traveling Book/Video Bag.)

Dear Parents:

Book Club is a great way to make reading an integral part of your family life. Four or more days per week, at least ten minutes a day, your child should spend quality time with a book, newspaper, or magazine. Quality time includes reading silently, reading orally, or, best of all, having someone read aloud to him or her! After reading, your child should record his/her minutes of time spent reading on a Book Club slip. Children should bring this slip into school, signed by an adult, at the beginning of each school week. The children will then tally their "reading" minutes on a calculator and keep track of their total reading time on their own individual classroom chart. This is a fun activity that shares their reading time at home with their classmates. It also uses mathematical skills to record progress.

Book Club

Here is how Book Club works:

- Your child reads at home for ten minutes or more. Record the time spent reading (orally, silently, or adult reading to child) in the box labeled "Number of Minutes," which may be found on the Book Club Weekly Recording Sheet.
- Read and record minutes for the entire week.
- Your child brings the Book Club Recording Sheet back to school on the first day of each week.
- Your child records his/her reading in increments of 100 minutes by adding stickers to his/her chart.
- For every 500 minutes recorded, your child can choose a free book. (Leftover minutes will be carried over to the next week.)
- Each child should be engaged in the reading process for at least forty minutes per week.
- This is a weekly homework assignment.

Reading to your child is the very best way to convince him/her that reading is a fun and valued family activity. Enjoy!

P.S. Look for "Bonus Book Club" opportunities in the classroom, too. Parents are welcome to visit and read to groups of children, in which case each child can add minutes to his/her chart.

Book Club Weekly Recording Sheet

For the week of: _April 9_ to _April 22_

Date Day	Monday	Tuesday	Wednesday	Thursday	Friday	Saturday	Sunday
Number of minutes	10	10	15	10	10	20	15

Student's name _Max_

Parent's signature _____

Students: Keep track of time spent reading each night. Your goal is to read for at least ten minutes a night for a total of forty reading minutes. Parents: Remember that reading to your child is the best way to gather minutes! More reading is always **appreciated**.

Book Club Weekly Recording Sheet

For the week of: _____ **to** _____

Date							
Day	Monday	Tuesday	Wednesday	Thursday	Friday	Saturday	Sunday
Number of minutes							

Student's name _____

Parent's signature _____

Students: Keep track of time spent reading each night. Your goal is to read for at least ten minutes a night for a total of forty reading minutes per week. Parents: Remember that reading to your child is the best way to gather minutes! More reading is *always* appreciated.

- -

Book Club Weekly Recording Sheet

For the week of: _____ **to** _____

Date							
Day	Monday	Tuesday	Wednesday	Thursday	Friday	Saturday	Sunday
Number of minutes							

Student's name _____

Parent's signature _____

Students: Keep track of time spent reading each night. Your goal is to read for at least ten minutes a night for a total of forty reading minutes per week. Parents: Remember that reading to your child is the best way to gather minutes! More reading is *always* appreciated.

Reproducible

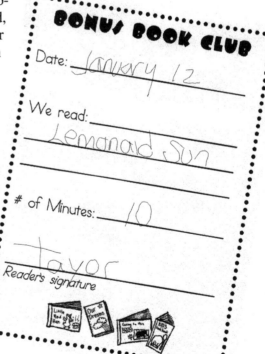

A Peek Inside Room 6

Volunteers and the Bonus Book Club

Encouraging students and their families to read at home is important. Unfortunately, some children do not have this opportunity. It was for this very reason that I started the Bonus Book Club.

Here's how it works: I select several theme-related stories and set them aside for volunteer readers. I also create a list of our reading clubs, which I store with these books. When a volunteer comes into the classroom, s/he takes a book and selects a club (e.g., a group of students who have been assigned to the same "club"). The volunteer reads aloud the book to this small group. The volunteer jots down the date and book title on the club sheet and the students record the number of minutes that the volunteer read to them on a recording sheet. These sheets are then added to the bucket where the students place their at-home reading recording sheets. In this way, every student will have minutes of reading to add to their yearlong totals. For every 100 minutes read, students record, with a sticker, on their own Book Club chart. For every 500 minutes of reading, the student may earn his/her very own book—for free! (See page 184 for Bonus Book Club reproducible.)

Note: You can create your own Bonus Book Club reproducible and include a picture or illustration that relates to your theme.

BONUS BOOK CLUB

Date: January 12

We read: Lemonaid Sun

# of Minutes: 10

Tayor
Reader's signature

BONUS BOOK CLUB

Date: _____

We read: _____

_____

_____

# of Minutes: _____

_____
Reader's signature

BONUS BOOK CLUB

Date: _____

We read: _____

_____

_____

# of Minutes: _____

_____
Reader's signature

BONUS BOOK CLUB

Date: _____

We read: _____

_____

_____

# of Minutes: _____

_____
Reader's signature

BONUS BOOK CLUB

Date: _____

We read: _____

_____

_____

# of Minutes: _____

_____
Reader's signature

Reproducible

Parent Conferences

Conferences are an important component of your teaching responsibilities. Help make these meetings upbeat and honest by providing a clear agenda, setting aside plenty of time for each meeting, keeping parents/guardians comfortable, and informing them of their child's progress within your educational program.

Schedules

When creating your conference schedule, leave plenty of time—approximately thirty minutes—for each conference. Longer conferences allow you and parents to chat informally and more comfortably when parents are not rushed. By lengthening conferences, however, you may have to schedule a few meetings before school, after school, or on a weekend.

For those parents waiting to conference with you, set up a comfortable waiting area, complete with chairs, class big books, and photo albums. In case you do run late, these items will keep parents occupied until you are ready to meet with them.

Informative and Upbeat Conferences

During each conference:
- Share the student's academic profile, but avoid child-to-child comparisons.
- Showcase his/her special talents.
- Discuss next steps.
- Show actual classroom artifacts. These provide a visual representation of the level at which the student is working. The more you can *show* parents, the better they will understand your verbal information.
- Share anecdotal stories—real stories about real classroom happenings.

Also share with parents specific assignments from the different curriculum areas. Provide examples of trade books, writing samples, math work, projects, and sample spelling screens. These items may be taken directly from the child's own individual assessment folder, which I suggest you update each day. (See Chapter 4 for more on assessment.) Share examples from the beginning of the year to the current moment as a means to showcase the child's *growth* rather than his/her *lack of growth*. Impress on parents exactly where their child currently stands within the developmental continuum areas of language arts and mathematics.

Question & Answer

Do you ever get behind schedule? If so, what do you do?

I schedule four conferences in a row, followed by a break. This way I know that I will catch up during the break time. The downside is that I usually don't get a break myself, but being able to give each parent—and in turn each child—the time they deserve is more important.

What does "developmental continuum" mean?

As teachers, we understand that children naturally learn certain things when they are developmentally ready. That means that even though we teach and reteach a certain skill, the student will make the skill his/her own only when s/he is ready.

Most developmental continuums are written in behavioral terms that define the attributes of each level within a learning area. Keep in mind that the levels to which I refer are not necessarily grade levels, they are the sequence of steps within academic learning. By writing these steps in behavioral terms I can clearly see where each of my students is working by comparing the continuum to the student's work samples and assessment pieces. I can then share this information with parents. This practice allows me to show what should be happening next for the student using these same kinds of behavioral descriptions.

For example, instead of simply saying to a parent, "Your daughter reads well," describe to them what that means in behavioral terms: "Your child can read a level E book for more than twenty minutes, and she can retell the story using great voice inflection. In addition, she recounts key story elements such as setting, character, plot development, and resolution." Now the parent knows at what instructional level his/her child can read, how long the child can sustain reading, and that the child understands what s/he is reading. The parent "sees" the behavior of a good reader.

Are students allowed to attend conferences with their parents? If so, does this change the tone of the conference?

Yes, in my school district students are invited to attend conferences with their parents/guardians. When students do attend, my "conference plan" remains the same: honestly and accurately relate and show what the child can do at present. The conversation should remain positive and should highlight, through student-work samples, where the student strives and where s/he needs more time to develop.

Question & Answer

I'm a school administrator and I would like some advice to share with my first-year and veteran teachers about how to conduct a successful conference.

This Q&A elaborates on some of the points mentioned in "Informative and Upbeat Conferences." First, explain to teachers, especially first-year teachers, that it is natural to be nervous about meeting with parents. Some conferences will inevitably be more challenging than others, and in order to make the experience a positive one for both teachers and parents, teachers should be as organized and prepared as possible. Suggest to teachers that they write down on paper the format for each parent conference. This plan might include the following components:

- Welcome parents and child, if present. (See previous Q&A.)

- Share with parents where their child began the year academically by showing student work samples.

- Share positive growth pieces and anecdotal notes (including student work samples). Make a list for each child that tells what steps the child has been taking and the progress s/he has been making in his/her develop-ment as a learner. These comments, by nature, are positive. I try to have actual classroom samples to back up the items on my list. I may have five to ten points that I want to highlight.

- Ask parents if they have noticed growth in their child.

- Share your "wish" for their child: "If there could be one area of improvement, it would be . . ."

    This exchange allows you to inform parents of areas in which their child needs to improve, but it keeps the

conference positive. No matter how far the student needs to go in order to improve, no parent wants to hear only negative comments. Always find something positive to point out.

- Ask parents what they "wish" academically for their child.

- Suggest books to read, games to play, and other activities on which parents and students can spend time together.

- Thank parents for sharing their child with you.

    At the end-of-year conference compare beginning-of-the-year samples with end-of-the-year samples to show parents how their child has grown.

Reading

Most parents of first graders are very concerned about their son/daughter's reading development. Share with them their child's progress in reading and emphasize the importance of reading with their son/daughter at home. In addition, share book titles their child has read, and look at the books together, discussing the type of literature that is appropriate for their son/daughter at this time. Assessment tools are also concrete indicators of where a student rates in a specific curriculum area; these indicators reinforce what you communicate with parents. (See Chapter 4 for more on assessment.)

Now, outline "next steps" for the student; share ideas with parents for how they can support and reinforce their child at home (e.g., fun literacy activities, reading); and before parents leave, in addition to the district report card, give them a copy of your remarks in narrative form about their son/daughter's progress. Informative articles that address the importance of reading at home or that contain fun family activities also make great handouts.

Finally, don't forget to keep notes from conference conversations, and highlight any questions they asked. These notes will remind you to contact the appropriate school professionals (e.g., Title I instructor, special education teacher, school psychologist, principal) about the conference, how the parents feel about their child's progress, questions, and possible next steps. For future parent conversations, also make note of any timelines you may have suggested. A word of advice: do not trust your memory. You will have so many conversations on these conference days that you will, without a doubt, need reminders.

Question & Answer

I always have some parents who don't sign up for conferences. How can I encourage them to attend?

There are many reasons why parents neglect to sign up for conferences; some are within your control (e.g., conference times), others are not. When asking parents to schedule a conference with you, consider these two questions:

- When do you schedule your conferences? Your district may provide a day during which you can hold them, but some parents are unable to take time off from work. For those parents who cannot meet during the day, provide morning and evening conference-time slots. You might even consider setting time aside for Saturday meetings.

- Does this conference mark the first time these parents have been into your classroom? Many parents are actually school-phobic due to their own negative school experiences. Beginning-of-the-year activities (e.g., Parents Night, Open House) can help them feel more comfortable with you and the school environment.

Post-Conference Reminders

Keep track of those parents with whom you meet, and write a follow-up letter to thank them for taking time out of their busy schedules to meet with you. For those parents who are unable to attend, send them their child's district report card and narrative report, and write a personal note letting them know that you missed meeting with them and hope to talk with them soon. This note is not a reprimand, but a second invitation.

Question & Answer

How do you keep track of these anecdotal notes during the conference?

I keep a folder filled with three-hole punch paper at my side for every conference. As I chat with parents, I write down key words. I will elaborate on these notes later and add this page to the student's binder section.

Volunteers

Volunteers in the classroom can be both a blessing and a hidden challenge. The bottom line is that you, your students, and the volunteers can benefit from extra support if routines, instruction, and tasks are clearly defined. (See Chapter 3 for more information on volunteers.)

Ask for volunteers in your summer newsletter and outline the many jobs that are available—from chaperoning to class helper. If you host a Parents Night, encourage parents to volunteer, and post a sign-up sheet to which potential volunteers can sign their names. Let all parents know, however, that they are always welcome in the classroom, that the door is always open. Thank them for any time they can give, and let them know how much you appreciate their help. Inform volunteers that there are often jobs that can be done at home, too, such as typing children's stories, sewing costumes or quilts, and even calling others for party and chaperoning needs. This will be the best—and the only—way for some busy parents to be part of the classroom.

As you begin to decide how parents or other community members can best help out in your room, brainstorm potential tasks volunteers could help with and when those tasks need to be completed. Make a list. Now, think about all the activities you would do if you had more time or more people to help you. Next, decide which of these activities you can "give away." You sometimes need to give up a little control in order to achieve more in the classroom.

Your list might include:

- Read stories to small groups of children
- Listen to children read
- Play math games/language arts games
- Plan a project for the class
- Help with spelling check-ins
- Listen to stories children have written
- Help with "messy" activities (cooking, crafts, etc.)
- Become a "room parent": organize classroom parties, etc.

- Produce the class newsletter
- Correct papers
- Teach a lesson
- Use flash cards with children
- Give math minute tests
- Photocopy
- Chaperone

Some volunteers like to be given a job with your expectations clearly outlined, others may like the challenge of planning an activity or just helping out in a more impromptu manner. Sometimes the very best service a volunteer can provide is listening to, reading with, or playing a game with a student(s). For some children, this could be a very big deal as their own home life may not lend itself to these kinds of experiences. I especially like to have volunteers read aloud to small groups of students, as all children should experience many and positive literature encounters with important adult role models.

Organizing Volunteers

Trying to organize these helpers does not have to be complicated. I use a copy of my weekly schedule and, in the appropriate time slot, write in the names of those parents/community members who can and want to volunteer every week. For these folks, I may ask them to take on a routine activity, such as the classroom newsletter, knowing that the students and I can count on them to do the job.

For those volunteers whose schedules are less predictable, I have created tubs of support activities and have included inside each tub a selection of games and/or books for volunteers to use. I have also included a set of laminated directions and a list of students the volunteer can work with for each activity. As volunteers meet with students they note the date or just check off the students' names. The next volunteer continues where the previous volunteer left off, following the same procedure. When these helpers arrive they know to check this tub.

What is nice about the above arrangement is that the procedure is uncomplicated—volunteers know the routine and I am able to continue with whatever I am doing without interruption. In addition, if a volunteer is unable to help out one week, students will simply continue with whatever they are working on at present. I try to schedule volunteers when students are pretty active, not sitting and listening to a whole-group lesson.

Question & Answer

How can volunteers be a hidden challenge?

Unless you have developed clear expectations for your helpers, you may find they need more guidance than you have time to give them. Therein lies the challenge: How to instruct volunteers while instructing students. It is possible, however, to instruct both at the same time when you address the class about the activity/activities with which volunteers will be helping.

A Volunteer Job: The Newsletter

Creating a classroom newsletter is not a difficult task, especially if you can enlist the help of volunteers. Not only do these volunteers provide a needed service, but by assisting in the classroom, they have more ownership over a finished product. Perhaps more importantly, they become community members who can directly advocate for the classroom educational program.

The classroom newsletter is a forum in which students can showcase everything that's taking place in the classroom. For instance, they might share

- classroom activities and word puzzles
- examples of content or lessons being taught
- news updates for parents

Create the classroom newsletter from the variety of print that covers your classroom walls and makes up student journals. This print might include recently written or read poems, a science experiment (as recorded in the children's science journals), or the weekly news announcements, complete with skills questions. Or how about discussing the novel students are reading aloud, or including a journal entry or two from the traveling book or movie journal? The possibilities are endless!

Class Newsletter

The Room 6 newsletter is published once a week. Which day it is published depends on my parent volunteers' schedules. One year it was published on a Friday, the next a Tuesday. The day does not matter, but issuing it once a week does. And because I don't issue "pencil-and-paper" work everyday, the newsletter is one of the primary ways parents find out what curriculum-related activities their students are involved with. It also serves as a means by which the class and I can remind parents of special school and classroom events and field trips. (See page 179 for more on "paper-and-pencil"/"drill-and-skill" homework.)

Our first newsletter of the year goes, without a title, to students' homes. In the first issue we ask students and parents alike for name suggestions. The rules for naming the paper are simple: the name must be related to our year's theme-study and should incorporate the name of a media venue (e.g., newspaper, magazine, press, etc.) Names are submitted, the class votes, and by the second week, our newsletter has a title.

Next, assign a small group of students to produce the newsletter for one month (one issue per week). The paper becomes their responsibility during the time block agreed upon, such as a free-choice time or a language arts time block. These children do not have to "make up" work; this is their work for that day.

Now, incorporate the print already in the room into your newsletter. During the first week of the newsletter, we brainstorm a list of all the print items available in the classroom, which includes:

- Poetry
- Traveling Book/Video journal entries (see page 152)
- News Share (see page 12)
- Minimal-cues messages (see pages 102-103)
- Money words
- Science journal entries (see page 126)
- Process-writing stories (i.e., stories in various stages of the writing process)
- Conversation journal entries (see page 107)
- Book dialogue journal entries (see page 107)

We also brainstorm another list of items students may want to write about. This list includes:

- Art class
- Library
- Read-alouds
- Classroom pet news
- Music class
- Field trips
- Upcoming events
- Physical education
- Theme-studies
- School news

I then laminate the list and keep it near the computer area for classroom volunteers to refer to each week.

The list may now also be used as a management piece. The volunteer(s) calls the newsletter group together and each child chooses two topics from the list on which to collect information, write about, or create for the week's newsletter. Volunteers help facilitate the collection process by typing information into the classroom computer. Once students have gathered the necessary information, volunteers work with their group on spelling, grammar, and punctuation. In Room 6

students usually watch volunteers type the newsletter into the computer. When the volunteer comes to a misspelled word, s/he points out the word and explains to students s/he will be typing it into the computer using the correct spelling. Sentence structure, however, remains in "kid" form.

Once the newsletter is completed, copies are made for students to take home. I also make copies for adults who have contact with my class, including the building administrator. With this knowledge people are aware of Room 6 happenings and can often dovetail their instruction with ours.

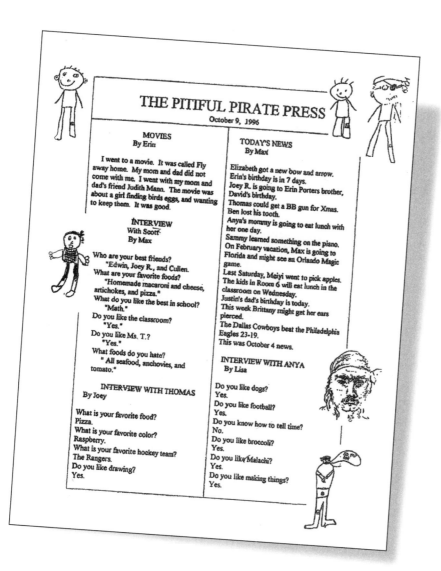

Illustrations on the newsletter correspond with our yearlong theme. During this particular year we were studying islands of the world.

COCO NUTS
By Lisa

What did the wall say to the ceiling?
Meet you at the corner.

Why didn't the skeleton go to the store?
Because he had no body to go with him.

MOVIES
By Joey

The class is watching a movie called "The Goonies". It is cool. It is about a pirate movie.

FIELD TRIP
By Anya

I like the field trip alot. We went on a ferry boat and then we went to Edwin's grandma's house and played there. Then we went back.

TRAVELING BOOKS
By Erin

I liked having the book Isla. It must be fun to fly around the world. A girl and her 'Abuela' visted a tropical Island.

MOVIES
By Anya

I like "The Sound of Music" alot and I like the songs alot. The first one is "The Hills are Alive" and the next one is "Do a Deer."

HOW TO KEEP YOUR SUBSTITUTE AS YOUR FRIEND

As much as you would like to think you will not need a substitute in your classroom, chances are you eventually will, and you need to be prepared. There is nothing worse than coming back from an illness or a teacher convention to a disgruntled administrator who has spent the previous day helping your substitute tame a wild class! Ensure a positive experience for your substitute and your students by guiding both through a day without you.

Communication Is Key:
Storage Ideas for Your Substitute Plans

Whether the substitute is new to your classroom or a familiar figure, it is important to create a comprehensive substitute folder or binder that includes information about your

- Instructional style
- Students
- Classroom and school environments
- Schedule
- Instructional time blocks
- Activities (including a good book to read with your class)

Often the folder/binder can be used from year to year with just a few minor changes. All you have to do is write a letter to your substitute (see pages 196-198) and the binder is ready to go. Your binder can also provide your school administrator with information about your students and your classroom program. Remember, communication is key!

Make sure you store your substitute binder in a place that is visible and easily accessible, as you want the substitute to locate and review the information before your class arrives. Also leave word with the school secretary as to where your binder can be found.

Question & Answer

I have seen "substitute folders" in school supply catalogs. Are they any good?

Yes, substitute folders provide places to write current information, and they have pockets to store schedules and extra plans. They work as a kind of outline/"sneak preview" to a more complete binder. Folders are available in most school supply catalogs, but two companies I suggest you try are Becky-Cardy and New England Supply.

Hello, Carol:

The kids had a ball the last time you were in the room, so they were really excited to hear you will be returning! Because you are somewhat familiar with our classroom routines, this letter will simply serve as an update about current room and school happenings.

As you know, students in all classes are preparing for our spring open house this Thursday evening. Because things are a bit hectic, I'm not sure if our music and gym classes are on their usual schedules. Just go with the flow and work with students on any tasks that need to be completed for open house.

You will have recess duty on Tuesday at 10:30 - 10:50 AM.

1. Throughout your stay specialists and volunteers will be in and out of the room. Just let them go about their business, but if you feel uneasy about anything or anyone, don't hesitate to contact the principal. Here's a list of visitors you will encounter:

- Mrs. Frizzle, the town librarian, will drop in around 10:00 AM on Monday for about 10 minutes. When you see her, gather the class at the rug, and when she is finished with her presentation (which is usually very good), have students return to what they were working on.

- Nan should be in to help out. I will leave her any unfinished "book making" and/or other small tidbits that need to get done before Wednesday night. If nothing is there, she should just "carry on." She knows what to do.

- Both Gloria and Nan come in on Tuesday. If you need help with anything or anybody, please ask them. They know the kids and what is expected, and they are very "cool."

- "Room Moms," Tina and, maybe, Astrid, will be in to work on the class newsletter with the students. They will do it all! Save me a copy of the newsletter and send the rest home with the kids.

2. You'll have an extra student in the morning. Ricky will be accompanied by his individual assistant, with whom I have pre-planned the day. She will help monitor his behavior and work. On both days, Ricky will leave before noon.

3. I will leave a list of kids who can help out in the kindergarten classroom. Having this outlet helps remind them to be on their best for you. (The kids and I devised this secret plan!)

4. Rob sometimes has a hard time with change, so try to "get him on your side" early by giving him a job or asking for his help. He is very sweet, but he sometimes gets sidetracked, especially when I'm not in the room. If he is having a hard time, please send him on an "errand" to the school secretary, the guidance counselor, or the librarian. Write a note that says: Could you find a job for Rob for a little while? The secretary, guidance counselor, and librarian all are great and will get him involved in something. Have them send him back to the room in thirty minutes or so. I think this will help avoid any unpleasant confrontations. No reprimands, please. Just divert him to this new setting; it really helps.

I think I am ready to start writing my plans! Yahoo! These plans outline our classroom routines, but if you have any other ideas or if the weather is just too good to be true, please follow your heart or your feet and take the class out for a dodge ball game or some other activity. (They have really been working hard for this open house!) Most of all, have fun with them! They are a special group!

Take care,

Ellen

Monday, April 1

Ahhhh, April Fool's Day. Keep an eye out for any tricks!

Please check my mailbox in the teacher's room for any notices that might need to be sent home with students. If you correct any papers, you can send those home, too. (Save math papers and knighthood booklets, as I need to record information from these.)

8:40 AM Students come in from the playground and start their FREE CHOICE TIME. (Write-up and routine are in the substitute binder.)

Students will situate themselves in the room. They should write in notebooks, and then choose a game to play. I will leave some puzzle-like sheets. You can pass these out to the whole class, save them for a "just-in-case" situation, or not use them at all.

Meanwhile . . . you need to do the LUNCH COUNT. Students will bring their money to you. You need to record it for the week, put the envelopes in the folder, and then tally the lunch count. Record in orange folder. Send money and the day's list of snack milk/juice recipients down to the kitchen with the "milk people." Send orange folder down to the office with the "messenger."

Set timer to ring for 9:40. Kids will gather at the rug area.

9:40-ish You get to sit in the "throne" (story chair)! Talk with students about how the day is going so far. Students should then start KNIGHTHOOD TIME.

Students are earning their knighthood by completing several individual theme-related contracts. (This is a year-long project.) Ask a few students (I'll leave a list) to share with you what they will be working on, although each student has a copy s/he can share with you if you have any questions. The class is so intent on becoming knights that their behavior for this time block has been exceptional! You could even extend this time or use it in another spot if it works for you.

Set timer to ring for 10:25. Students should meet at the rug.

While students are busy working independently you can concentrate on any "crowd control" issues.

10:30 RECESS! Dismiss students for recess.

10:50 Students come in from recess.

Meet the class at the rug area. Have them begin READING TIME. I may leave a word puzzle for them to do first. Check on table. I will label it for you. During this time students will read, work on book projects, and write in their response journals. Usually they have a conference with me, but tell them we'll hold conferences when I return.

Set timer to ring for 11:55-ish. Time to pick up and get ready for lunch.

12:05-12:45 PM LUNCH is followed by a 20-minute RECESS.

12:45 Students in from recess. Meet at the rug area for **TRAVELING BOOKS** time. Kids will lead this activity. One student will share a book and then choose someone to take the book home that day.

12:55 STORY TIME! I have left two books on the table: *Good Grizelle* and *The Girl in the Golden Bower*. Choose one to read on Monday and the other on Tuesday.

1:30-ish SILENT READING for 15 minutes. Set timer to ring.

1:45 Students gather at the rug area for **MATH TIME.**

We have been working with pattern blocks. At this point I am trying to reinforce the names of the shapes.

Try to get the kids to use the real names, and have them play this game:

MIMIC-A-SHAPE

I have made game boards for this activity. Students will each need a game board. Directions are on the game board.

We have only recently started playing this game, so you will still need to model it for them. When I play this with students, I have them trace their design, then write the value for it using the letters written in the shapes. A design might have 1H + 2Z + 4A +1R.

Once you model with the class, you can have them try it with partners. Why don't you go ahead and pair students by pulling names out of a hat.

If this activity does not take up the whole time, have students work on their "regular" math work. They will know what that means. (Routine for math time is in the substitute binder.)

2:50-ish. Set timer to ring for pick up.

Students should get ready for home. Buses will be called. Stack chairs at the end of the day (kids will do this; just remind them).

Day 1 is all done! Go home and relax. Day 2 is coming up!

APRIL 2

8:40 FREE CHOICE TIME for students, **LUNCH COUNT** for you

9:40 MUSIC Students need to be there in concert order. I will leave the list of order in this mass of papers!

10:25 Music ends

10:30 RECESS . . . YOU'RE ON DUTY!

10:50 KEYWORD TIME

We have not done this in a while, but the class loves it. Kids will write and illustrate during this time. When they are ready, students will come to you for a "new" word. You write it on an index card for them. Ask them to share their old word and writing with you first. If you think they could do more, ask them to. (There is a longer write-up of this activity in the back of the substitute folder.)

11:55 Set timer to ring. Students will gather at the rug area.

12:05 - 12:45 PM LUNCH/RECESS

12:45 TRAVELING BOOKS

   STORY TIME

   SILENT READING 10 minutes

1:15 PM KNIGHTHOOD TIME

Set timer to ring for 1:55, at which point students should meet at the rug.

2:00 Begin "regular" math time. The routine for this is in the substitute binder. Some students may be working on math papers. When they are done with these they should follow the routine by choosing a math game to play. You can play, too!

2:55-ish Get ready for buses. Pass out any papers. Stack chairs.
You made it!!! Thanks so much. Do let me know if there were any difficulties.

Part I: Instructional Style

Write a one-page description of what the room should sound and look like during independent and other work times. Also, explain what kinds of behavior-management systems you use when students misbehave. This is extremely important. There is nothing more disconcerting for your class than to have a substitute teacher change all the rules on them. A class that is used to being able to chat quietly, for example, will be confused and potentially unruly if silence suddenly becomes the order of the day in your absence.

Part II: You Know Your Students Best

Describe the class makeup. Leave tips about which children work well together, which do not, and which have special needs. In addition, inform your substitute about which students will need to leave the room to meet with specialists and which will need to visit the nurse for their medication.

Part III: Classroom Environment

Include a schematic of your classroom. Identify important areas of the room such as the bathroom, gathering area, computers, and whatever else might be mentioned in the plans. Also include a copy of your classroom job chart. Imagine the response a substitute would have if s/he chooses the "wrong" child to lead the line!

CLASSROOM ENVIRONMENT

ROOM 6 STUDENTS

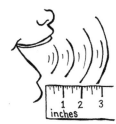

There are twenty-one students in Room 6. They range in abilities and temperaments, but overall, they work very well together. They adore listening to stories. And I like to give them some extra time outside to pla a game and run off a little of their energy!

When students work independently, it's fine for them to talk as long a they use their "3-inch" voices! (A "3-inch" voice is a voice you can only hear three inches away!)

INSTRUCTIONAL STYLE

Instructional style is so personal that it's difficult to begin to describe my own, except to say that my strength as an educator lies in my ability to "step off" center stage. That is, I don't always have to be the "director" for learning to happen in the classroom. In fact, the most powerful learning happens when we—students, parents, and myself—work alongside one another.

Part IV: School Environment

Introduce your substitute to school policies and the names of other professionals in your building (nurse, principal, specialists, and teachers). You should also include fire drill information and the school's discipline policy. Make a note as to where recess is held, what the playground rules are, and what is expected of teachers while on duty. I put a copy of the school's handbook in this section, too.

Part V: Weekly Schedule

Make sure your schedule clearly states those important "other" times during the school day such as lunchtime, duty times, and specialist times.

Part VI: Instructional Time Blocks

Describe the different time blocks listed on your weekly schedule. (See Chapter 5 for more on curriculum routines.) If your class runs on routines, your students, who know these routines better than anyone, will help guide the substitute through the day. If you know you are going to be absent, I suggest you write out the day's schedule for your substitute and place it at the front of your substitute binder (Hint: purchase a binder with a clear pocket front. This makes your schedule visible and easily accessible.)

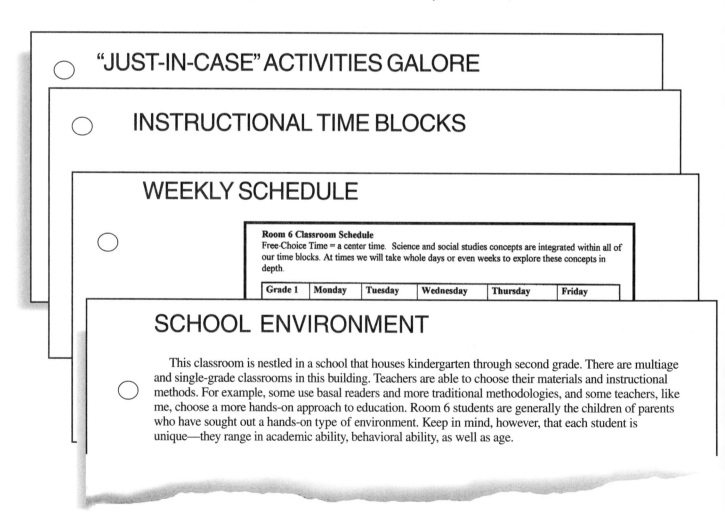

"JUST-IN-CASE" ACTIVITIES GALORE

INSTRUCTIONAL TIME BLOCKS

WEEKLY SCHEDULE

Room 6 Classroom Schedule
Free-Choice Time = a center time. Science and social studies concepts are integrated within all of our time blocks. At times we will take whole days or even weeks to explore these concepts in depth.

Grade 1	Monday	Tuesday	Wednesday	Thursday	Friday

SCHOOL ENVIRONMENT

This classroom is nestled in a school that houses kindergarten through second grade. There are multiage and single-grade classrooms in this building. Teachers are able to choose their materials and instructional methods. For example, some use basal readers and more traditional methodologies, and some teachers, like me, choose a more hands-on approach to education. Room 6 students are generally the children of parents who have sought out a hands-on type of environment. Keep in mind, however, that each student is unique—they range in academic ability, behavioral ability, as well as age.

Part VII: "Just-in-Case" Activities Galore!

Some substitutes will come to your classroom with their own bag of tricks, but it's always good to keep on hand activities guaranteed to succeed. So if all else fails, this section will come to your substitute's rescue! Leave complete plans for language arts, math, and theme-related activities. And as mentioned, include a book for the substitute to read with students. Make it perfectly clear that it is okay to use any of these activities, as they are all relevant to your curriculum.

Here's a sample of some of the activities I have left for my substitutes.

***Anti-Coloring Book* (series),** by Susan Striker (Henery Holt and Company. Check out Barns and Nobel— www.bn.com — for various titles.) Most coloring books force children to stay within already constructed lines. The Anti-Coloring Book series, however, provides images in which some of the lines are pre-drawn and some are not. This activity, therefore, allows students to use their imaginations and determine their own boundaries.

Photocopy and include three or four of these pictures in your substitute binder. Students can each choose their own page to work on, or the entire class can draw the same picture. After students have completed their pictures, they can share their responses to the provided reading prompt. (This series is available in most bookstores.)

Videos: Videos should never simply be used to pacify students, but they can provide a substitute with a little peace and quiet—time to regroup or prepare for the next lesson. If you include a video as an optional activity, take care to select quality programs from companies such as Scholastic, Trumpet, Wonderworks, Eyewitness, Early Advantage Programs for Children, Hi-Tops Video, and Lorimar Home Video. If you don't own your own classroom copy of these titles, recommend the following names and video-production groups to your librarian.

- The *I Spy* video shows how the popular I Spy books by Jean Marzolla are created. Students love these books, and the video is sure to spark post-viewing questions and conversations. Students might even be inspired to create their own I Spy pictures. I suggest you have the substitute read one of these books before s/he shows the video. (Scholastic, 30 minutes. ISBN: 0-590-93606-9)

- *Mercer Mayer's Three Stories* tells about the author and three of his "Little Critter" books. (Golden Book Video: Storybooks Brought to Life. ISBN: 0-307-13861-5)

- Students can visit with Mem Fox, a well-loved award-winning children's book author, in *Trumpet Video Visits*: Mem Fox. Look for other author titles, too. (Trumpet Video Visits series)

- *Reptile*, one of ten books in the Eyewitness book/video series, is sure to appeal to your first graders. (Eyewitness, 35 minutes. ISBN: 1-56458-918-8.)

- *Gryphon*, by Charles Baxter, is based on the short story of the same name. This video retells the experiences of a very special substitute who works in a city school. (The Wonderworks Family Movie series has produced a variety of films based on children's literature titles, many of which appear on children's television. Each feature is approximately one hour in length. ISBN: 0-7800-0115-X)

- *Five Stories for the Young*, by Weston Woods, is part of the Children's Circle Video

Reading Program. The video relays these five popular stories using their original book illustrations. (Early Advantage Programs for Children. ISBN: 6302820898)

- *Madeline*, narrated by actor Christopher Plummer, also uses the original book illustrations to retell the story of this irresistible young lady. (Hi-Tops Video. ISBN: 1-55873-432-5)

- *Beverly Cleary's Ramona: Mystery Meal and Rainy Sunday* brings a 3D Ramona and her escapades to life. (Lorimar Home Video, 60 minutes)

A Peek Inside Room 6

A Few Classroom-Tested Activities

The Greedy Triangle: This clever book by Marilyn Burns will keep students thinking as they create a "greedy triangle" book of their own. (See page 203 for the step-by-step activity directions. ISBN: 0590489917)

Glasses, Who Needs 'Em? Written by Lane Smith, this book is sure to get your students thinking about all those creatures that, if human, would need glasses (e.g., a skunk or a raccoon). Students have fun picturing these creatures with glasses perched on their noses and are eager to depict just how these creatures might appear. (See page 204 for step-by-step activity directions. ISBN: 0670841609)

Quick As a Cricket (ISBN: 0859531511), by Audrey Wood, is a wonderful book that introduces children to the concept of opposites through the use of similes (e.g., I am as fat as a pig. I am as thin as a lizard).

Beautifully illustrated by the author's husband, Audrey Wood addresses opposites through her central character, a young boy, who experiences many contrasting feelings throughout the course of the story. Add various animals to the mix and you have a book guaranteed to capture the interest of your first graders. (See page 205 for step-by-step activity directions. ISBN: 0859531511)

The Greedy Triangle

Skills
- Understanding the concept of triangle as a geometric shape
- Ability to locate triangles in both linear and solid form within the environment

Materials
- *The Greedy Triangle*, by Marilyn Burns
- White construction paper (for book pages)
- Various-sized pre-cut triangles
- Form sentence strips (see page below)
- Markers
- Crayons
- Glue

Directions
1. Read the book *The Greedy Triangle*.

2. Using white construction paper, pre-cut triangles into all different sizes. In addition, photocopy a sheet with the form sentence reproducible: "A _____ has a triangle." Leave these form-sentence strips together with the pre-cut triangles.

3. Instruct the substitute to take the class for a walk around the school, inside and outside, in search of objects that contain triangular shapes.

4. Once back in the classroom, students use markers and crayons to recreate a picture of an object they identified as containing a triangular shape. (They can use the white construction paper to draw on.) Students then choose from the pile of different-sized, pre-cut triangle pieces and glue one that is similar in size into their picture.

5. Students should now take a form-sentence strip, write the name of their object in the blank space, and glue it onto their picture.

6. If time allows, the students can bind their individual pictures into one class big book. (See page 000 for directions on how to bind pages into a class big book.)

A _____ has a triangle.

Glasses, Who Needs 'Em?

Skills
- Use of imagination to brainstorm and draw a creature who needs glasses
- Copying animal name from chart
- Creating a background picture for the creature

Materials
- *Glasses, Who Needs 'Em?* by Lane Smith
- Construction paper
- Form sentence strips (see page below)
- Construction paper glass frames (available through some teacher supply catalogs)
- Pipe cleaners

Directions

1. After the substitute reads the story, the class should brainstorm a list of creatures who "need" glasses.

2. Students can now select a creature they would like to draw on the construction paper.

3. Photocopy the form sentence: "A _____ needs glasses, that's who!" reproducible page. Students can write the name of their creature in the blank space and paste it onto their picture.

4. If time allows, have the substitute and the students bind pictures together into a class big book. (See page 000 for directions on how to bind pages into a class big book.)

Adaptation

Beforehand, construct enough pairs of construction-paper glass frames for each student in your room. With a paper punch, punch a hole on either side of the frames. Now, insert a pipe cleaner through each of the holes and gently twist. Have available lots of cool "stuff" (e.g., multicolored glitter, stickers, colored paper, etc.) with which children can decorate their frames.

- -

A _____ needs glasses, that's who!

Reproducible

Quick As a Cricket

Skills

- Learning about, brainstorming, and using opposites in writing and drawing
- Learning about and creating similes
- Adding the appropriate background information to illustrations

Materials

Quick As a Cricket, by Audrey Wood   Construction paper cut into 12" x 12" squares
Markers/crayons   Form sentence strips (see page below)

Directions

1. Read the book *Quick As a Cricket*.

2. Discuss the central character's feelings. Ask students if they have ever felt the way the character feels. Talk about what similes are and why people use them in writing and speaking.

3. Brainstorm a list of opposites. Now brainstorm a list of animals to showcase each opposite.

4. Give each student a template that models the book's language and format, then ask students to draw two pictures. On one side of the two-page spread, students fill in their first sentence, each showcasing their word pair: I am as _____ as a _____.
On the second page of the two-page spread (the facing page), students fill in the opposite pair:
I am as _____ as a _____.

   For example:

   I am as fat as a pig.   I am as thin as a lizard.

5. From the list of opposites the class has brainstormed, students select one or more opposite adjective pairs (fast/slow; fat/thin; tall/short) and the animal(s) that corresponds (e.g., rabbit/turtle; pig/lizard; giraffe/armadillo).

6. Students now fill in the blank lines with their opposite pair and show their work to you (the substitute) who writes the text, spelling words correctly, at the bottom of the two pieces of 12" x 12" construction paper.

7. Students then illustrate both sentences, making sure they place themselves into the picture along with the animals they have chosen.

8. Now, gather the pictures and bind them into a class big book, making sure each student's two pages are facing one another. (See page 13 for directions on how to bind pages into a class big book.)

"Quick as a Cricket is published by Child's Play Inc., Maine. www.childs-play.com."

- -

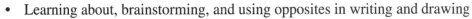

I am as _____ as a _____.

I am as _____ as a _____.

Reproducible

Student Behavior with the Substitute

I have begun to believe all children are born with a "let's-get-the-substitute" gene. I used to think it only showed up in older students, but I know from personal experience that it is quite alive in the younger ones, too. It is important to consider this added challenge when preparing for your substitute.

Dedicate a class meeting at the beginning of the year to talk about appropriate behavior for when a substitute teacher or any other guest visits your room. Your students most likely know the difference between appropriate and inappropriate behavior, but they might find it very difficult not to be silly when someone else is present. Acknowledge this, but together brainstorm ways students can help one another maintain control, and explain that they need to try their best, and that is what counts.

In addition, discuss with students possible consequences for breaking the "try" rule. These reprimands should not be scary or unrealistic, but communicating with students about the consequences is essential. In other words, don't surprise them with a punishment. They need to know up front what inappropriate behavior will result in. Often students will decide that the appropriate response to poor behavior with a substitute is to write him/her an apologetic note or card. This note should be written during students' free time.

Taking a Break

For children who have a hard time connecting with others, or for those who are naturally mischievous, design a substitute plan that will allow them to curb their behavior before they get into trouble—allow them to "take a break." For example, one student might help out in the office for a short while, while another may read to a kindergarten class. Now instead of feeling crummy about the day, these students can feel good about helping other folks in the building.

Post-Substitute Meeting

When I return to the room, we hold a "good stuff/bad stuff" conversation during our normal class meeting. Here the class shares how the previous day went, and I am constantly amazed by how honest they are about their behavior. Students don't use names, but behavior difficulties are discussed in depth, and together we talk about what needs to be improved—whether it be behavior or lesson plans—for the next time a substitute visits the room. The idea of "taking a break," for example, came out of one of these meetings.

In addition, Room 6 students have articulated which time blocks are the hardest for them to manage, such as when the substitute tries to "be me" during news shares or conference times. As a result, and unless s/he is a respected "veteran of Room 6," I rarely ask the substitute to replicate these parts of the day.

Of course, it is also important to encourage substitutes to leave their impressions of their experience with your class, whether they write notes in the margins of your daily plans or a reflective letter. Whatever the format, ask them to provide you with more than just a "list of offenders." While this information is also important, it's more helpful to find out about the successful and the more challenging parts of their day.

If you are lucky, you will find a substitute who matches your classroom style and who will want to come back again and again. When the substitute really becomes part of the program, the impact of your absence is diminished and your class will function as smoothly as if you were there.

Directions and Diagrams

Flower Box Storage and Display Boxes for Your Classroom

Note: Underlined words are defined in the Glossary of Building Terms.

The "flower box" concept is a simple and fun method for storing and displaying books in your classroom. What's great is that if you cut the pieces ahead of time, the box construction is easy enough so that you can involve your students in its assembly. The materials and construction directions below are for a 4' (L) x 12" (W) x 4" (H) flower box; however, you may custom design your own flower box to fit on the furniture in your classroom.

I recommend you build these boxes at home. If you are unfamiliar with such woodworking, ask someone who is handy in this field to help you out. If you decide to finish assembly at school, however, consider inviting a local builder or craftsperson—perhaps one of your students' parents—to aid in assembling the storage boxes. Remember to have the craftsperson explain and demonstrate safety during assembly. Invite the craftsperson to stay after construction for a Q&A session about his/her work. This is a great way to involve the community in your classroom!

Materials

· 1" x 4" pine lumber (length of lumber depends on number of boxes and dividers you are going to make.) The 1" refers to the wood's thickness, if you were to lay it down flat; the 4" refers to the wood's width—or the wood's height—if you were to stand it on edge. (In this example, the flower box structure will be 4" high.) *Actually, the thickness is closer to ¾", not 1", but it's still referred to as 1" x 4" lumber. Refer to flower box schematic.

· 1 sheet of plywood

· Approximately 42 6 <u>penny</u> nails or <u>Sheetrock screws</u>

· hammer

· non-toxic paint, stain, or polyurethane

Construction

Sides (considered the length of the box, which is 4'): Cut 1 x 4 lumber into two 4' lengths.

Ends (considered the width of the box, which is 1'): From a piece of 1 x 4 lumber:

· Cut two 10½" lengths. *You are cutting 10½" segments because once you fit the ends inside the sides, you will see that each side's width measures ¾". The two sides' ¾" segments adds up to 1½". Together with the length of the end board—10½"—they add up to 1'.

Dividers (width=10½"):

· Determine how many dividers you want along the 4' length.

· Now determine how far apart you want them to be spaced from one another (determine   spacing by measuring the width of a "typical" book. As your classroom might contain books of different widths, you should consider having dividers separated into two or more sections of different measurements.)

Assembly

· Stand one of the ends up vertically and align the side so that it is flush with the end (see the accompanying diagram). Fasten this joint with two or three nails (6 penny nails) or several Sheetrock screws. If screws are used, you may want to predrill starter holes to eliminate splitting.

· Nail the other end in place, then mark the location of the dividers (In this example I spaced the dividers apart by 6"-7".) You can leave one or two spaces more than 7" for larger books, as is shown on the flower box diagram in this example.

· Nail the dividers to the same side you nailed the ends.

· Turn the entire assembly over and nail on the other side, again using two or three nails at every joint.

Bottom: At the lumberyard, have a ¼" thick piece of plywood cut into a 1' x 4' rectangle. Then, using small nails (I suggest <u>flooring nails</u>), nail the plywood into the frame of your flower box structure. A bottom will allow you to move the box—books and all—without having to remove anything first!

Decoration: With your students, paint, stain, or polyurethane your flower box. I love to use fun and vibrant colors for different boxes, but you may want to stain or polyurethane your boxes all the same color. After you have decorated your box, place it on a table or bookcase, and fill it full of books!

How to Build a Step Table

A step table is a piece of furniture you and your students can use for lots of things. Students can use it as a table, a quiet place to sit and read, or when several are in a group, they can use them as "risers" for singing or playacting.

Note: Underlined words are defined in the Glossary of Building Terms.

A step table should be made from:

- 3/4" finish plywood. Birch veneer works well. It has a solid wood core and a thinveneer of birch wood on both sides. It is primarily used in making cabinets. It can be stained, painted, or just protected with several coats of polyurethane. (Whatever finish you put on the finished product should be "child safe.")

- Birch veneer plywood is about $50.00 for a 4 x 8 sheet.

- You will need two sheets for this project.

The most critical part in the entire process is cutting the pieces from the two sheets of plywood (cutting diagrams for both plywood pieces included). Most of the cuts are simple straight cuts that can be done with a handheld electric saw. The angled cut between the two sides (what will become both the left and right inner and outer sides of the step table) can be done with a saber saw (a powered jigsaw).

- After marking the line for the angle (see diagram), carefully cut ON the line; that is, bisect the two pieces exactly. (Normally woodworkers mark a cutting line and cut just to the edge of the line—but not for this operation.)

To ease the assembly of this project, all joints are <u>lap joints</u>. If you want to reduce the amount of exposed end-grain rabbit joints, miter joints could be used; however, you would have to augment the exact dimensions of the pieces to accommodate this change. (This type of change should be made by an experienced wood worker.)

Next:

· Glue and fasten all joints with either finishing nails or flat head wood screws. If you use finishing nails, set them (using a nail set) so that the head is below the surface of the wood.

· Fill the hole with wood putty and sand before finishing.

If you fasten the pieces with flat head wood screws:

· <u>Countersink</u> (v) the holes prior to driving the screws so you can fill them before finishing.

You can change the exact placement for the inner sides and the upper and lower shelves to accommodate specific uses. For example, you can buy long, narrow, plastic boxes and slide them into the upper shelf area. These boxes become "drawers," which provide a place for drawing utensils or other classroom materials.

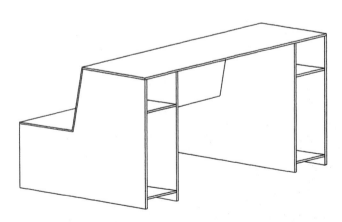

Step Table: Plywood Cutting Diagram-Plywood Sheet 1

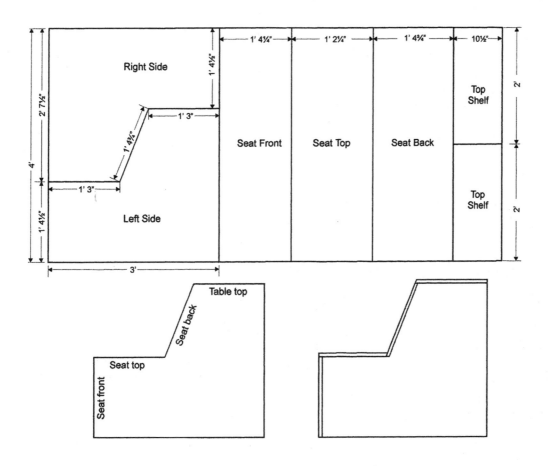

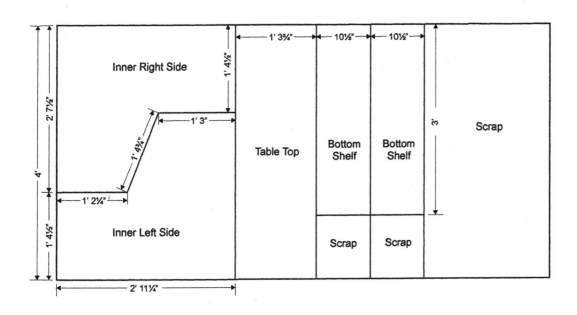

Step Table: Plywood Cutting Diagram-Sheet 2

How to Build a Classroom Loft

General Information

A classroom loft utilizes space well and provides a great place for students to work and perform.

Safety and strength should be your first priority when constructing a loft, and it is strongly suggested that you consult with a competent craftsman (preferably one designated by your school or district) for review of theses directions prior to construction of the loft. Before this project even begins, however, you must receive permission to build the loft from your school principal, who should consult with district and school building and safety codes.*

Please also note that most of the work involved in the construction of a loft will be easier if at least two people are working on the project. Attaching the legs is actually much easier if three people are working together.

These directions are for a loft consisting of

- two 4' x 8' platform sections, pieced together to form an "L" shape
- 5' clearance
- 3/4" thick plywood floor
- 1/4" thick carpet
- 24 ¼" (length of) railing above the deck

The upper area of the loft (the deck) will be surrounded by railings, covered with carpeting, and will be accessible by ladder.

These platform sections can be modified for a smaller loft or a loft that better meets the standards-safety and otherwise-for your room; however, in order to ensure proper and safe construction, it is strongly suggested you consult with a competent craftsman before and after changing dimensions.

A glossary of woodworking terms, a complete bill of materials, a tool list, several detailed drawings, and general construction notes are all included.

General Notes

- Don't hesitate to ask lumberyard or hardware store employees any questions about tools or materials.
- Most views of the loft presented in the following pages show the top view of the loft. For that reason, some details are hidden or are not shown in each view.
- Do not use pressure treated wood when constructing your loft. Pressure treated wood is impregnated with several chemicals for rot resistance, one chemical of which is arsenic.
- Countersink all carriage-bolt nuts. Bolts should not extend beyond the surface of the wood.

Based on the author's construction of a loft in her classroom, these materials and construction directions, if followed correctly, will build a strong, safe loft. However, neither the author nor the publisher makes any express or implied warranties concerning such materials or construction directions, and neither shall be liable under any circumstances for personal injuries or property damage resulting from construction or use of a loft.

Classroom Loft: Bill of Materials

Note: Underlined words are defined in the Glossary of Building Terms, pp.   .

The approximate cost of materials for a loft consisting of two 4' x 8' long platforms, as presented in these plans, will be approximately $400.00.

Frame and Deck

Quantity	Description	Size
3	2 x 4 (lumber)	8'
1	2 x 4	7' 10 ½"
13	2 x 4	45"
1	2 x 4	46 ½"
56	16 penny nails	
2	sheets of plywood-smooth one side	3/4" (thick)
1	box of flooring nails	
4	31/4" carriage bolts-with nuts and washers	
1	box of chicken wire staples or large tacks for fastening carpet to plywood	
	carpet-short-pile (1/4" thick) is better, as it is easier to clean	
	carpet pad *If you decide to use a carpet pad, adjust the height of the railing supports (the part of the leg above the deck) accordingly.	

Legs and Railing Posts

Quantity	Description	Size
15	2 x 4	7' 5"
		*Allows for a 5' clearance below the loft. Above is a 3/4" (thick) plywood deck covered in a ¼" (thick) carpet. Railings rise 24 ½" above plywood deck.
1	2 x 6	7' 5"
1	2 x 4	2' 5"
22	3 ¼" carriage bolts (with nuts and washers)	
36	16 penny nails	

Railings

1	box of 1 3/4" Sheetrock screws (you will need at least 64 screws)	
4	1 x 4	1' pine boards
8	1 x 4	4' pine boards
8	1 x 4	8' pine boards
4	1 x 4	12' pine boards

Note: The railing lengths listed above are approximate. Measure for exact fit.

Ladder

Quantity	Description
2	2 x 6 Pine boards for the ladder sides. The length of these sides will depend on the height of the deck and the specific angle desired for the ladder. (See diagrams.)
5	2 x 6 Pine for the ladder steps. You could use 2 x 4 material for the steps if desired. You may find that you want four or six steps, depending on the height of the loft deck and the rise desired between each step. The rise of each step should be between 10" and 12".
1	box of 3 ½" Sheetrock screws (at least 30 are needed for five steps)
2	2 x 3 Pine for railings (one on each side of the ladder)
2	2 x 4 3' post for lower end of railing

Miscellaneous

Pillows: for comfortable reading

Boxes: for holding books

Tools Needed

· 2 hammers, including 1 framing hammer

· Electric drill

· Drill bits: a conventional twist drill for carriage bolt holes (probably ¼") and another (probably a spade drill with a 1" diameter) for counter-sinking the holes for the nuts and washers.

Measure the shank of the carriage bolts and the diameter of the washers for exact dimensions. As carriage bolts have a smooth, round head, the hole for the shank of the bolt should be only slightly larger than the bolt diameter. This will allow the square portion of the bolt (under the head) to grab into the wood as you drive the bolt in and hold it from turning as you tighten the nut.

· Ratchet and socket set: for tightening the carriage bolts.

· Wood saw (electric): preferably an electric handheld saw if the work is to be done in the classroom. If some of the initial work can be done outside of the classroom, use a radial arm or a table saw.

· Wood saw (handsaw)

· Phillips screw driver, or Phillips driver bit for an electric drill, as you will be driving a multitude of screws.

· Wood block plane: for running a chamfer along the edges of all materials used in the construction to eliminate sharp corners and edges.

· Wood chisel: for cleaning out the dados for the ladder steps. (A radial arm saw can make these easier and faster; however, if one is not available, cut the sides with a handheld electric saw, and then clean out between the saw cuts with a chisel.)

Classroom Loft: General Directions

The Decks

Note: Refer to the **Loft Frame Construction** diagram for additional details.

The decks (floor of the loft) are each composed of a 4' x 8' piece of ¾" plywood, reinforced by floor joists and surrounded by a framework, composed of 2 x 4s. You will eventually form an L-shaped loft, composed of these two frame/deck structures.

Note that after you have constructed the two loft deck frames, you will attach plywood to the framework, smooth side down (as you will ultimately cover the upper surface with carpet). And that after you have assembled the frame, all 2 x 4s (both the floor joists and the 8' long side pieces) will be on their edge (i.e., all pieces of the framework are assembled so that when finished the 4" end-grain side is vertical.) Refer to the diagram for clarification if needed.

Now, start with the simplest deck structure, which is composed of two 8' 2 x 4s boards.

·   Cut seven 2 x 4s 45" long. These will become the floor joists for the plywood floor.

·   Start at one end of the 8' board and nail it into the end grain of the first 45" floor joist, using a simple lap joint. It is normal woodworking practice to use nails that are at least three times the thickness of the wood through which the nail will pass when attaching one piece to another. A normal 2 x 4 is 1½" thick (2" prior to surface finishing). This means the nails for the framework should be around 3½" in length. 16 penny nails will fit this criteria.

·   Pound two nails into the ends of each floor joist.

·   Attach another joist at the opposite end of the 8' 2 x 4. Again, use two nails for this joist.

·   Place the remaining joists along the length of the 8' 2 x 4 at 16" intervals. Try to keep the floor joists located at 16" on center, as you will be able to easily nail the flooring to them when their location is identified.

Once you have nailed all the flooring joists to one 8' side (of the 2 x 4), turn the entire assembly over and nail on the other side.

Construction for the second deck is similar, but slightly different. The only difference is that you should:

·   Overlap the floor joist with the side frame in one corner. This is done so that the 2 x 6 leg that is attached at that point will be stronger. Due to the difference in one corner of this part of the loft frame, one side piece will be 8' long and the other will be 7' 10½" long. One floor joist will be 46'½", and the remainder (six of them) will be 45" long. Consult the diagram for further explanation of this difference in this corner construction. As before, you should space the floor joists on 16" centers. Also, similar to the other half of the loft, you should orient all 2 x 4s so that the 4" side (of the 2 x 4) is vertical when completed.

·   Once you have completed both 4 x 8 loft frames, lay them flat on the floor and nail on the ¾" plywood. Use flooring nails for this. These nails are serrated along their shank. The shank grips the wood into which you are hammering, thereby reducing the chance that the nail will ever become loose.

The Legs

Note: Refer to the **Loft Leg Construction and Placement** diagram for additional details.

All the legs for the loft are 7' 5" long. Below the deck surface this piece of wood a leg. Above the surface of the deck this same piece of wood doubles as a support for the railings. You will attach the deck to the legs at a height so that the bottom of the deck is 5' from the floor. (In other words, when the loft is completed, there will be a 5' clearance between the bottom of the deck and the classroom floor.) There should be 24¾" or more above the deck (between deck and the top of the railing support) to allow for a ¼" carpet and 24½" high railings.

(At this height the top of the top rail, when you add it later on, will be <u>flush</u> with the top of the support. If you raise of lower the height of the loft or choose a carpet thicker than ¼", you will need to adjust the length of the legs accordingly.)

The corner legs (one inside corner and five outside corners) are composed of two 2 x 4s, which you should nail together.

To put these corner legs together:

· Lay one of the 7' 5" 2 x 4s on the floor so that the 4" side is vertical.

· Place another 7' 5" 2 x 4 flat on top of it so that one edge is even (flush).

· Now, consult the **Loft Leg Construction and Placement** diagram for a top view of how to assemble corner legs.

· Nail the second 2 x 4 in place with at least one nail every 10" (these nails run the length of the corner legs). You should again use nails approximately 3½" long.

· Assemble all six corner legs. The other legs are simply a single 2 x 4 cut to a length of 7'5". Place these at the middle of the 8' span for extra support and strength.

Attaching the Legs to the Decks

Note: Refer to the **Loft Leg Construction diagram** for additional details.

Once you have assembled the two decks and have put together the six corner legs, you can attach the legs and stand the deck up.

To do this:

· Start by standing one of the two deck assemblies on edge.

· Lay down one corner leg and adjust it so there is exactly 5' extending below the bottom surface of the frame.

· Hold the leg in that position and drill (using an electric drill with a ¼' ' drill bit) a hole completely through the leg and the 2 x 4 frame. If necessary, you can use a clamp (a <u>C-clamp</u> will work) to hold the leg in this position for drilling. The diameter of this drill bit should be the same as (or only slightly larger than) the shaft diameter of the <u>carriage bolts</u> that you will use to attach the leg to the frame.

· Drill only one hole at this point. You will eventually drill a second hole, but if you drill two holes at once there is more of a chance the leg will slip out of position and the holes will not line up when installing the bolts.

· Remove the drill and place the leg aside temporarily.

· Using a spade drill, (with a width slightly larger than the diameter of the washer being used on the carriage bolts) drill a counter-sink on the inside of the frame. This counter-sink should be ½" deep.

· Replace the leg and drive a carriage bolt, starting from the outside, into the hole in the leg, and going through the leg and through the 2 x 4 frame.

The square portion of the shank of the bolt, just below the head, will sink into the wood of the leg and prevent it from turning. The smooth head will protrude only slightly and will not create a safety hazard.

Next:
· Place a washer and a nut on the inside of this carriage bolt and tighten with a ratchet socket- driver and socket.

· Once this bolt is tight drill a second ¼" hole (below the first one), countersink the inside, drive a second carriage bolt into this hole and tighten with a washer nut as before. (Remember: If you drill two holes at once there is more of a chance the leg will slip out of position and the holes will not line up when installing the bolts.) The exact placement of the holes will depend on the placement of the nails you used to attach the long deck frame to the floor joists. Consult the front view, as depicted in the **Loft Railing Construction** diagram, for the approximate placement of the bolts that hold the legs to the deck. Notice that the bolts on the corner legs are placed one above the other. The bolts on the single 2 x 4 legs (those at the middle of the 8' span) are placed to the left and to the right of the 2 x 4 deck floor joist, located at this point.

· Continue placing the legs around the deck, first drilling one hole in each leg, counter sinking the inside, and tightening one bolt.

Once you have installed the first bolt in a leg, it is easy to drill, countersink, install, and tighten the second bolt. And once you have assembled all the corner legs and have installed the single 2 x 4 legs, you should be able to stand the loft upright. After you have attached the legs to both sections, you can connect them together.

To connect the two sections together:
· Move the two sections together and drill the hole for the first bolt from one frame to the other, as is shown in the **Loft Frame Construction** diagram.

· Countersink this hole as you did when you attached the legs to the frame, and install and tighten the first bolt. Once this bolt is in place, the remaining three holes can be drilled. Countersink these holes and install the bolts.

Now that the two deck sections are connected, you can install the last leg (2 x 6). This leg is held by four carriage bolts, two on either side of the 2 x 4s that are in that position. Refer to the **Loft Leg Construction and Placement** diagram for the position of this 2 x 6 leg.

Carpet Installation
Now that the loft is standing and the two sections have been connected together, you can install the carpet. This should be done **prior to installing the railing**, as the bottom rail will cover and hold down the edge of the carpet. The height of the legs above the ¾" plywood flooring material is such that a ¼" carpet can be installed and have the appropriate length for the railing.

· Cut the carpet to fit the plywood deck. Use small staples or large upholstery tacks to hold the carpet down.

· Place the staples/tacks around the perimeter of the carpet. When the first piece of railing is installed it will also hold down the edge of the carpet and cover the tacks or staples you just drove in.

Short Uprights

Note: Refer to the **Loft Leg Construction and Placement** diagram for additional details.

Depending on the design of your loft, you will have either one or two short 2 x 4 upright sections that you will need to attach. One of these uprights, if you install it, will add additional support to the railings. The other short upright support is used as one side of the opening for the ladder.

To place this short upright:

· First determine the overall width of the ladder that you will be building. The opening for the ladder should be the same as this width.

· Cut the short uprights to a length of 29" and attach to the loft framework with carriage bolts so that the bottom is flush with the bottom of the deck frame. Chamfer the bottom edges of these supports to reduce the chance of injury.

The Railing

Note: Refer to the **Loft Railing Construction diagram** for additional details.

The railing around the upper portion of the loft is composed of four lengths of 1 x 4 pine boards, which you should attach horizontally. The exact dimension of a 1 x 4 board is closer to ¾" x 3½". The spacing between the four railing boards is 3 ½". The upper portion of the supporting legs should measure 24½" above the carpet. (This length allows for is the total width of four 3½" high railing pieces (with three 3½" spacing between railings).

Refer to the **Loft Railing Construction** plans to determine which railing sides need to be installed first. Pay careful attention to the diagrams. These plans will allow you to have the greatest surface area to fasten the railing boards.

For installation:

· Cut the railing boards to the appropriate length and chamfer the edges.

· Pre-drill the holes in the railing boards and fasten to the uprights with 1½" Sheetrock screws. You must pre-drill the holes, as they are close to the end of the railing boards, which the screws will split if you do not pre-drill the holes. You should use a drill that has a diameter slightly smaller than the diameter of the shank of the screws.

· Now, place the bottom railing directly on top of the carpet that you tacked down in a previous step.

· After attaching the bottom rail, use several scrap pieces of the same railing material as a spacer to determine the height of the second piece of railing.

· Pre-drill the holes in this piece of railing and attach it to the uprights.

- Take out the spacers and use them again for the third piece of railing.

- Finish out the railing on that side by placing the top board flush with the top of the uprights and, after pre-drilling the holes, attach it in place with 1½" Sheetrock screws. That should complete the railing on one side of the loft.

- Continue attaching the railing on another side of the loft starting with the bottom piece first and working up to the top.

- Attach the remaining pieces of railing material, remembering to leave an opening for the ladder.

Ladder Construction

Note: Refer to the top and side view of the **Loft Ladder Construction** diagrams for additional details.

The sides of the ladder are made from two 2 x 6s. You will cut the 2 x 6s at an angle on the bottom so they rest flat against the floor. Cut them at a complementary angle at the top so you can fasten them to the loft itself.

The ladder should meet the loft deck at an angle of between 30° and 40°. It should be steeper than a set of stairs, which are usually more than 50°. The exact measurements of the ladder on your loft will depend on the angle desired, the height of the loft deck, the step <u>rise</u>, the width desired, and other factors. Several methods for determining some of these measurements are described below.

One way to find the length of the ladder sides is to stretch a string from the top of the deck surface to the floor at a desired angle. You can use a protractor to determine the angle. Once you have identified the appropriate dimension for your loft, you can measure the length of the string. (You could also use a steel carpenters tape measure if it were held tight (straight) and not allowed to droop.)

When you create the ladder, remember the old woodworkers maxim "measure twice; cut once." If you are comfortable using simple math techniques you can also use some of that trigonometry you learned in high school to determine some of the ladder dimensions. (If you decide on a 30° angle for the ladder, some of the formula elements have been computed for you below.)

Here's what to do:

- Measure the deck height from the floor to the top of the plywood. The length of a 30° angle ladder would be 1.154 times that measurement. You can test the measurement by stretching a string from the top of the loft deck to the floor at the angle desired and then measuring the length of that string. This will double check the length for the ladder side prior to cutting.

- If the deck height is for a ladder at this angle, cut the lower end of the ladder side at a 60° angle and the top end at a 30° angle. Use a protractor to determine these angles.

- Lay out the bottom 60° angle and make the first cut for the base of the ladder. This cut will eventually lay flat on the floor. Consult the **Loft Ladder Construction** (front view) to see the cut angles of this piece of the ladder side.

- The upper angle for this ladder would be 30°. Lay this out with a protractor and cut the ladder side to the proper length.

The multiplier for a ladder of 30° degrees is 1.154. This multiplier is found by taking the reciprocal of the cosine of the ladder angle (1/cos a). The multipliers for other typical angles are listed below.

Angle	Multiplier
20°	1.064
25	1.103
30	1.154
35	1.221
40	1.305
45	1.414

If you construct a ladder different from the one described in these directions, cut it at angle (X). The cut for the bottom angle would be 90° - (X)° . For example, the bottom cut on the ladder side piece would be 55° for a ladder that meets the deck at 35°.

Once you have cut both sides of the ladder and have determined the sides will fit in place correctly, then it is time to cut the <u>dado</u> for the steps. These dados are square-bottomed grooves into which you will eventually fit the ladder steps.

Dado Background Notes: You will eventually place dados so that the rise of the ladder steps is between 10" and 12". If the loft clearance is 5', the total deck height off the floor will be 5' 4½" or 64½". If you place five steps on the ladder, the rise will be exactly 10¾". (If you are constructing a loft of a different height, compute the number of steps necessary on your ladder so they are approximately 10"-12" apart.)

You will then cut the dados into the ladder sides at a depth of ½" at the same angle as the cut at the bottom of the ladder side. The ladder steps will then be parallel to the floor.

You will then place the end of the step into the dado cut in the side of the ladder. It provides much greater strength than just butting the end of the step against the flat surface of the ladder side.

Once dados are cut into both sides you will be able to cut the step "treads" (another term for "steps") to the appropriate length.

Finally, you will pre-drill the holes for attaching the treads and screw them in place with 3" long Sheetrock screws.

To mark and cut dado locations:

- Start with one side of the ladder. Make sure you have cut the top and bottom angles on this piece and have checked that it fits when placed against the loft in the proper position.

- Lay the ladder side on your work area. Again, if your loft has a clearance of 5' and a total deck height of 64½", you will find that you can have five steps with an equal rise of 10¾".

- Carefully measure (at a 90° angle) from the bottom on the ladder side the rise distance minus the tread thickness. (Tread—or step—thickness= 1½")

The bottom surface is that surface that will ultimately be placed against the floor. The first step will be 9¼" from the floor. The 9¼" + 1½" (tread thickness)= a total rise of 10¾".

At this point:

- Draw a line on the ladder side parallel to the bottom surface from which you just measured from. For a ladder that meets the loft at 30°, draw that line at an angle of 60° (just like the cut at the bottom of the ladder side).

· Draw another parallel line 1½" from that line. These two lines, 1½" apart, mark the edges for the first dado that you will eventually cut into the ladder side. The step material, cut from a 2 x 6, is actually 1½" thick and will just slide into this dado when it is cut.

From the second line that you just marked (which is 10¾" from the bottom surface):

· Measure (again at a 90° angle from the line) up another 9¼". At this point draw a line parallel to all the others (at 60° for a ladder that meets the loft at 30°).

· Again, like for the first dado, draw another parallel line 1½" from the one you just drew.
Proceed to the other end of the ladder side with this same process.

· First measure out and draw a line 9¼" from the last line drawn and then draw another parallel line 1½" from that one.

· When all step dados are marked hold the ladder side in place again just to check the spacing of the steps. The top step should end up 10¾" from the deck surface.

You can cut the sides of the dado with a handsaw; however, a handheld electric saw makes cutting much easier. Either way, do not cut deeper than ½" into the ladder side.

To cut:

· Set the electric saw blade depth at ½".

· Carefully cut along the inside of each dado line. Remember, these lines are 1½" apart—the same as the thickness of the treads.

The saw blade has a width of 1/8". If you cut on the outside of the lines, you have added an extra ¼" width to the dado and the step, which, when placed in the dado, will be very loose.

Once you have cut the two edge cuts for each dado:

· Cut out the center with a chisel. Sometimes it helps if you make several cuts between the two dado edges in order to loosen the wood between the sides. This makes cleaning out the groove with a chisel easier.

After you have cut the dados into one side of the ladder, use these grooves to mark the locations for the dados on the other side of the ladder. Remember, you will have a right and left side for the ladder. Don't make the two sides exactly the same. One should be just the opposite of the other. Once marked and the lines drawn, cut the dados in the other ladder side.

Previously, when you installed the railings around the upper portion of the loft you left a space for the ladder to be placed. This ladder opening will have a specific width. The tread length is dependent on this opening width. If you place the ladder sides against the sides of the leg and short upright as shown in the **Loft Ladder Construction** (top view) diagram, the treads will be 2" shorter than the opening. This allows for ½" of each end of the step treads to be inserted into the dados in the ladder sides.

Now:

· Cut the required number of step treads from a 2 x 6.

· Pre-drill holes in the ladder sides for the 3½" Sheetrock screws that are used to hold each step.

· Use three screws in each end of the steps. Insert these into the end grain of the step from the outside surface of the ladder side.

Optional Skirt Around the Bottom of the Loft

The completed loft should be sturdy; however, it should also be fastened to the wall for extra safety. If you find that it still wiggles slightly you can add some additional strength by placing a skirt, composed of 1 x 6 boards, around the base of the loft. Add the skirt on the back and sides of the loft first, as it is advantageous to leave to the front of the loft open so that children can move easily in and out of the area under the deck.

Place bookshelves, pillows, or small desks below the loft deck. Students can use the upper part of the loft for reading and other quiet activities. It can also be used, with a screen hung over the railing, for puppet shows.

Glossary of Building Terms

16" on center: Normally the spacing of both floor joists, rafters, and wall studs is such so their centers are at intervals of 16"—also known as 16" on center.

Boards: Unlike dimensional lumber, which is at least 2" thick, boards are usually about ¾" thick. Boards usually come from the sawmill 1" thick, but when planed, or smoothed, the thickness is reduced to ¾".

C-clamp: A C-clamp is a wood clamp shaped like the letter C. It has a single screw, usually with a small handle, used to tighten the clamp. A C-clamp can be used to temporarily hold two pieces of wood when drilling an assembly hole.

Carriage bolt: A carriage bolt is a bolt with a rounded head. A square portion of the bolt shaft directly under the head "bites" into the construction material so that the bolt will not turn when tightened.

Chamfer: A chamfer is a beveled surface at an edge or corner. It is used to soften a sharp 90° edge on a piece of wood to reduce the chance of injury.

Counter-sink (n): A counter-sink is a recess in the surface of the construction material so that a bolt, nut, or screw head will sit below the surface when installed. Countersinking (v) this hardware reduces the possibility of injury.

Dado: A dado is a square-sided channel cut into the flat surface of a piece of wood. It is primarily used to give additional strength to two boards attached at a 90° angle.

Dimensional lumber: Local lumber dealers often speak of dimensional lumber. This term is used to collectively describe construction materials that have a thickness of at least 2" (e.g., 2 x 4s, 2 x 6s, and 2 x 10s).

Flooring nails: These serrated nails contain small nicks along their edges. These nicks bite into the material being nailed and hold tighter than would a smooth nail.

Flush: When two pieces of wood are placed so that their edges, are even they are said to be flush.

Framing hammer: A framing hammer is heavier than a normal household hammer. You can drive large nails better with a framing hammer.

Joist: A floor in a house is supported by pieces of wood, usually spaced 16" apart. These supporting pieces of wood are called joists.

Penny: This is a shortened term, derived from the word pennyweight. In medieval times the weight of a silver penny was used to measure precious metals and gems. Today, one use of this term is for the weight—or more often thought of as the size—of nails. A 20 penny nail, for example, weighs "20 pennyweights," and subsequently, is much larger than a 10 penny nail.

Phillips screwdriver: A Phillips screwdriver has a small x-shaped point at the tip. This type of screwdriver is used on Sheetrock screws.

Phillips screwdriver bit: A bit that can be placed in the chuck of a power drill, turning it into a power screwdriver. Using this bit will make your work much easier!

Pilot holes: A hole in the construction material slightly smaller and shorter than the shank of the hardware that will ultimately be driven into the hold. Use of pilot holes will eliminate the construction material from being split during assembly.

Ratchet and socket set: Normally, a ratchet and socket set are considered mechanics tools. The socket is like a small cup that surrounds a nut when it is being tightened. The ratchet is the handle for the socket and allows you to quickly tighten the bolts on the loft.

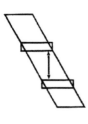

Rise: When relating to stairs and steps, rise is the vertical distance from the top surface of one step to the top surface of the next step. For stairs this rise is usually between 6"-7". The normal rise of ladder rungs is about 12". You must consider the age of the students who will be using the ladder on the loft to determine an appropriate rise. Through trial and error it was determined that a rise of only 6"-7" on the loft ladder was too small. As the angle for the loft ladder was steeper than a set of stairs and more closely resembled a normal ladder, a rise of around 10" was found to be more appropriate.

Sheetrock screws: Sheetrock screws are course-threaded, flat head screws normally used to hold Sheetrock or plasterboard to the wall <u>studs</u> during the construction of a house. They also make perfect hardware for the assembly of wood construction. <u>Pilot holes</u> should be pre-drilled first so the wood does not split when the screw is driven.

Studs: Pieces of <u>dimensional lumber</u> used as the support for house walls Studs are usually either 2 x 4 or 2 x 6. When shopping for loft materials you may find the 2 x 4s listed as studs. As wall studs are ultimately hidden behind other wall materials they are often rough and sometimes twisted or crooked. Select studs that are as straight and smooth as possible.

Spade drill: A spade drill has a sharpened flat cutting surface at the end of a round pencil shaped shank. It is usually used in an electric drill. A spade drill is used to create the counter-sink for the nuts and washers on the carriage bolts that hold the legs of the loft to the deck. Select one that has a cutting width slightly larger than the diameter of the washers you are using.

Treated wood: Pressure treated wood is impregnated with several chemicals for rot resistance. One of these chemicals is arsenic. DO NOT use pressure treated wood for any part of loft construction.

Twist drill: A twist drill (or conventional drill) has screw like grooves cut along ½ to ¾ of its length and is sharpened at one end. It is usually used in an electric drill.

Loft Frame Construction
(Top View)

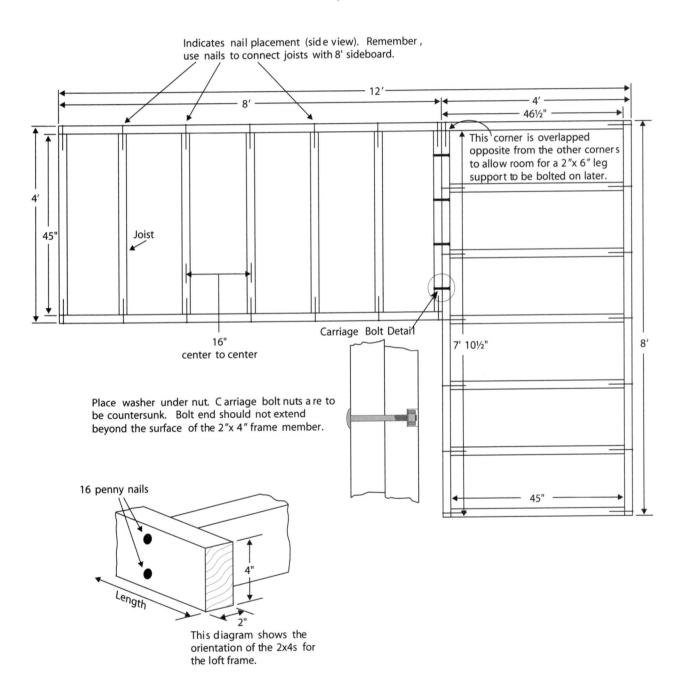

Indicates nail placement (side view). Remember, use nails to connect joists with 8' sideboard.

12'

8'

4'

46½"

This corner is overlapped opposite from the other corners to allow room for a 2"x 6" leg support to be bolted on later.

4'

45"

Joist

8'

16"
center to center

Carriage Bolt Detail

7' 10½"

Place washer under nut. Carriage bolt nuts are to be countersunk. Bolt end should not extend beyond the surface of the 2"x 4" frame member.

45"

16 penny nails

4"

Length

2"

This diagram shows the orientation of the 2x4s for the loft frame.

Loft Leg Construction and Placement
(Top View)

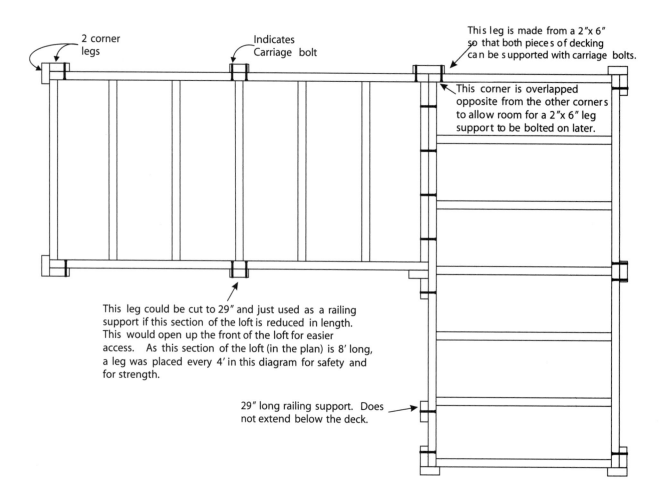

2 corner legs

Indicates Carriage bolt

This leg is made from a 2"x 6" so that both pieces of decking can be supported with carriage bolts.

This corner is overlapped opposite from the other corners to allow room for a 2"x 6" leg support to be bolted on later.

This leg could be cut to 29" and just used as a railing support if this section of the loft is reduced in length. This would open up the front of the loft for easier access. As this section of the loft (in the plan) is 8' long, a leg was placed every 4' in this diagram for safety and for strength.

29" long railing support. Does not extend below the deck.

Loft Railing Construction
(Top View)

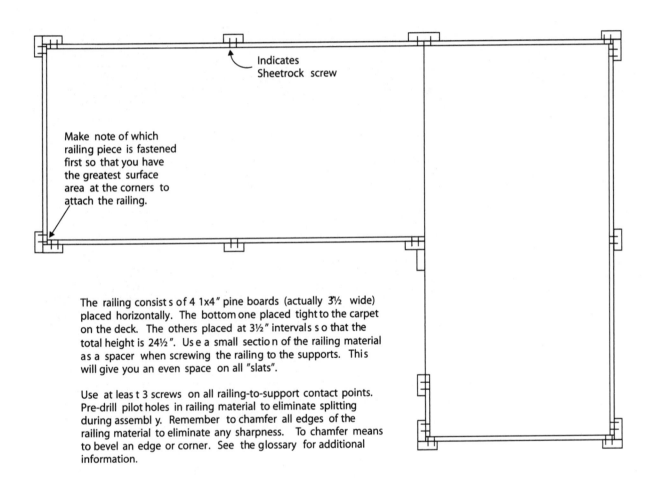

Indicates
Sheetrock screw

Make note of which
railing piece is fastened
first so that you have
the greatest surface
area at the corners to
attach the railing.

The railing consists of 4 1x4" pine boards (actually 3½ wide)
placed horizontally. The bottom one placed tight to the carpet
on the deck. The others placed at 3½" intervals so that the
total height is 24½". Use a small section of the railing material
as a spacer when screwing the railing to the supports. This
will give you an even space on all "slats".

Use at least 3 screws on all railing-to-support contact points.
Pre-drill pilot holes in railing material to eliminate splitting
during assembly. Remember to chamfer all edges of the
railing material to eliminate any sharpness. To chamfer means
to bevel an edge or corner. See the glossary for additional
information.

Loft Ladder Construction
(Front View)

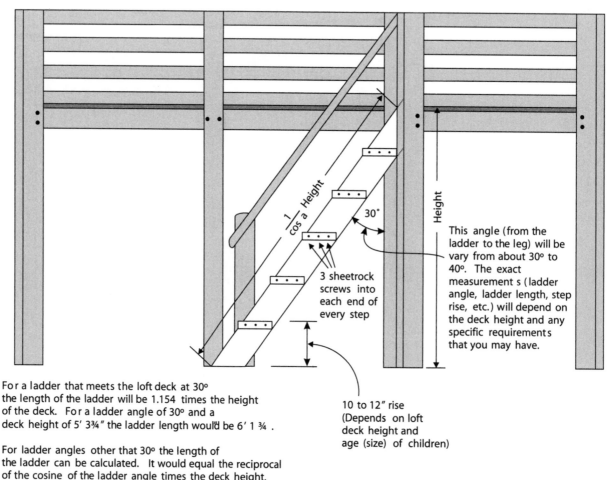

$\dfrac{1}{\cos a}$ Height

30°

Height

3 sheetrock
screws into
each end of
every step

This angle (from the
ladder to the leg) will be
vary from about 30° to
40°. The exact
measurement s (ladder
angle, ladder length, step
rise, etc.) will depend on
the deck height and any
specific requirements
that you may have.

For a ladder that meets the loft deck at 30°
the length of the ladder will be 1.154 times the height
of the deck. For a ladder angle of 30° and a
deck height of 5' 3¾" the ladder length would be 6' 1 ¾ .

For ladder angles other that 30° the length of
the ladder can be calculated. It would equal the reciprocal
of the cosine of the ladder angle times the deck height.

$\dfrac{1}{\cos a}$ Height

The accompanying text provides alternative methods for
finding the length of the ladder.

10 to 12" rise
(Depends on loft
deck height and
age (size) of children)

Bottom of ladder
side, cut at 60°

Top of ladder side,
cut at 30°

½" deep dados cut at
same angle as bottom

Loft Ladder Construction
(Top View)

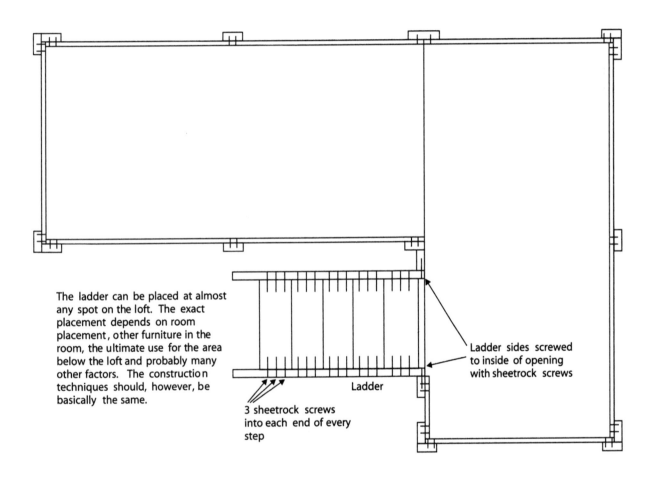

The ladder can be placed at almost any spot on the loft. The exact placement depends on room placement, other furniture in the room, the ultimate use for the area below the loft and probably many other factors. The construction techniques should, however, be basically the same.

3 sheetrock screws into each end of every step

Ladder

Ladder sides screwed to inside of opening with sheetrock screws

Loft Ladder Construction
(Detail)

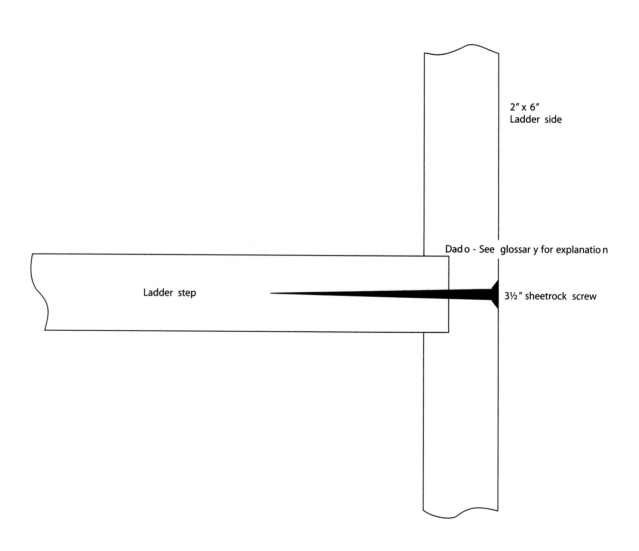

2″ x 6″
Ladder side

Dado - See glossar y for explanatio n

Ladder step

3½″ sheetrock screw

Recommended Resources

Learning Centers

BOOKS

Blevins, Wiley. *Quick-and-Easy Learning Games: Phonics.* New York: Scholastic, 1996.

Gregory, Cynde. *Quick and Easy Learning Centers: Writing.* New York: Scholastic, 1995.

Holliman, Linda. *The Complete Guide to Classroom Centers: Hundreds of Ideas That Really Work.* Cypress, Calif.: Creative Teaching Press, 1996.

Ingraham, Phoebe Bell. *Creating and Managing Learning Centers: A Thematic Approach.* Peterborough, N.H.: Crystal Springs Books, 1997.

Isbell, Rebecca. *The Complete Learning Center Book.* Beltsville, Md.: Gryphon House, 1995.

Kanter, Patsy. *Quick and Easy Learning Centers: Math.* New York: Scholastic, 1995.

Kepler, Lynne. *Quick and Easy Learning Centers: Science.* New York: Scholastic, 1995.

MacDonald, Sharon. *Colors.* Contact Crystal Springs Books at 1-800-321-0401 for ordering information.

—. *Squish, Sort, Paint, and Build.* Beltsville, Md.: Gryphon House, 1996.

McMillan, Dana. *Center Time: The Complete Guide to Learning Centers.* Carthage, Ill.: Teaching and Learning Company, 1995.

Opitz, Michael. *Learning Centers: Getting Them Started and Keeping Them Going.* New York: Scholastic, 1995.

Spann, Mary Beth. *Quick and Easy Learning Centers: Word Play.* New York: Scholastic, 1995.

MAGAZINES

The Mailbox® Magazine
PO Box 51676
Boulder, CO 80323-1676
(800) 627-8579
www.themailbox.com

MATERIALS

Finger Pointers and PVC pipes are available through Crystal Springs Books (www.crystalsprings.com). See "Educational Publishers" for address information.

Brain-Based Learning

Kaufeldt, Martha. *Begin with the Brain: Orchestrating the Learner-Centered Classroom.* Tucson, Ariz.: Zephyr Press, 1999.

Behavior

Kohn, Alfie. *Beyond Discipline: From Compliance to Community.* Alexandria, Va.: ASCD, 1997.

—. *Punished by Rewards: The Trouble with Gold Stars, Incentive Plans, A's Praise, and Other Bribes.* Portsmouth, N.H.: Heinemann, 1993.

Assessment

BOOKS

Atwell, Nancie. *In the Middle: New Understandings About Writers, Readers, and Learning.* Portsmouth, N.H.: Heinemann, 1987.

Beaver, Joetta. *Developmental Reading Assessment: DRA Student Folders.* Reading, Mass.: Celebration Press, 1999.

Bird, Lois Bridges, Yetta Goodman, and Kenneth S. Goodman. *The Whole Language Catalog: Forms for Authentic Assessment.* New York: McGraw Hill, 1997.

Bolton, Diane, and Faye Bolton. *Teaching Spelling: A Practical Resource.* Portsmouth, N.H.: Heinemann, 1993.

Bridges, Lois. *Assessment: Continuous Learning.* Portland, Maine: Stenhouse Publishers, 1995.

Buchanan, Ethel. *Spelling for Whole Language Classrooms.* Katonah, N.Y.: Richard C. Owens, Publishers, 1989.

Clay, Marie M. *The Early Detection of Reading Difficulties.* Portsmouth, N.H.: Heinemann, 1990.

Campbell Hill, Bonnie, Cynthia Ruptic, and Lisa Norwick. *Classroom Based Assessment.* Norwood, Mass.: Christopher-Gordon Publishers, 1998.

Coletta, Anthony. *What's Best for Kids: A Guide to Developmentally Appropriate Practices for Teachers and Parents of Children Ages 4-8.* Rosewood, N.J.: Modern Learning Press, 1996.

Fiderer, Adele. *Practical Assessments for Literature-Based Reading Classrooms.* New York: Scholastic, 1995.

Goodman, Gretchen. *Inclusive Classrooms from A to Z: A Handbook for Teachers.* Columbus, Ohio: Teachers' Publishing Group, 1994.

—. *The Whole Language Evaluation Book.* Portsmouth, N.H.: Heinemann, 1989.

Grant, Jim, and Bob Johnson. *The First Grade Readiness Checklist.* Peterborough, N.H.: Crystal Springs Books, 1997.

Grant, Jim, and Irv Richardson. *The Retention/Promotion Checklist (K-8).* Peterborough, NH: Crystal Springs Books, 1998.

Hansen, Jane. *When Writers Read.* Portsmouth, N.H.: Heinemann, 1990.

Harp, Bill, ed. *Assessment and Evaluation in Whole Language Programs.* Norwood, Mass.: Christopher-Gordon, 1993.

Gillet, Jean Wallace, and Charles Temple. *Understanding Reading Problems: Assessment and Instruction.* Reading, Mass.: Addison Wesley Longman, 1999.

International Reading Association and the National Council of Teachers of English. *Standards for the English Language Arts.* United States: IRA and NCTE, 1996.

Johnston, Peter. *Constructive Literacy Assessment.* York, Maine: Stenhouse Publishers, 1997.

—. *Running Records: A Self-Tutoring Guide* (audio). Portland, Maine: Stenhouse Publishers, 2000.

Kendall, John S., and Robert J. Marzano. *Content Knowledge: A Compendium of Standards and Benchmarks for K-12 Education.* Aurora, Colo., 2000.

McDonald, Heather. *Self-Assessment-Starters: Activities to Promote Reflective Learning.* Mountain View, Calif.: Creative Publications, 1998.

NAEYC. *Developmentally Appropriate Practice in Early Childhood Programs.* Revised. Washington, D.C.: NAEYC, 1997.

National Research Council. *National Science Education Standards.* Washington, D.C.: National Academy Press, 1995.

Picciotto, Linda Pierce. *Evaluation: A Team Effort.* New York: Scholastic, 1992.

Rhodes, Lynn K. ed. *Literacy Assessment: A Handbook of Instruments.* Portsmouth, N.H.: Heinemann, 1993.

Routman, Regie. *Invitations: Changing As Teachers and Learners (K-12).* Portsmouth, N.H.: Heinemann, 1991.

Snowball, Diane, and Faye Bolton. *Spelling K-8: Planning and Teaching.* Portland, Maine: Stenhouse Publishers, 1999.

Wood, Chip. *Yardsticks: Children in the Classroom Ages 4-14: A Resource for Parents and Teachers.* Greenfield, Mass.: Northeast Foundation for Children, 1997.

Zgonc, Yvette. *Sounds in Action: Phonological Awareness Activities and Assessment.* Peterborough, NH: Crystal Springs Books, 2000.

Websites

The Achieve website links you to the governor's office and state department of education for all fifty states: www.achieve.org

Math Exemplars for K-2 students: www.exemplars.com

Curriculum

Books

Allen, Margaret. Various phonics titles are available through Crystal Springs Books (www.crystalsprings.com). See "Educational Publishers" for address information.

Bauer, Karen, and Rosa Drew. *Alternatives to Worksheets: Motivational Reading and Writing Activities Across the Curriculum.* Cypress, Calif.: Creative Teaching Press, 1992.

Carlile, Candy. *Book Report Big Top.* Cypress, Calif.: Creative Teaching Press, 1980.

Gentry, Richard. *Teaching Kids to Spell.* New York: Scholastic, 1996.

Hall, Nancy, and Rena Price. *Explode the Code* (series) Cambridge, Mass.: Educational Publishing Service. Check out Barnes & Noble (www.bn.com) for various titles.

Hiatt, Catherine, Doug Wolven, Gwen Botka, and Jennifer Richmond. *More Alternatives to Worksheets: Motivational Reading and Writing Activities Across the Curriculum.* Cypress, Calif.: Creative Teaching Press, 1994.

Klawitter, Pamela Amick. *Book Report Beagle.* Cypress, Calif.: Creative Teaching Press, 1994.

Lieberman, Lillian. *File Folders for Math Plus.* Palo Alto, Calif.: Monday Morning Books, 1999.

—. *File Folders for Phonics Plus.* Palo Alto., Calif.: Monday Morning Books, 1999.

McCarrier, Andrea, Irene C. Fountas, and Gay Su Pinnell. *Interactive Writing: How Language and Literacy Come Together (K-2).* Portsmouth, N.H.: Heinemann, 2000.

McCracken, Marlene J. and Robert A. *Spelling Through Phonics.* Winnipeg, Manitoba: Peguis Publishers, 1997.

Novelli, Joan, and Judy Meagher. Interactive Bulletin Boards: Language Arts. New York: Scholastic, 1998.

—. *Interactive Bulletin Boards: September to June.* New York: Scholastic, 1998.

—. *Interactive Bulletin Boards: Math.* New York: Scholastic, 1998.

Pinnell, Gay Su, and Irene Fontas. *Guided Reading: Good First Teaching for All Children.* Portsmouth, N.H.: Heinemann, 1996.

WEBSITES

Four Blocks™

Teachers.Net Four Blocks Center: www.teachers.net/
4blocks

Four Blocks Chatboard: www.teachers.net/mentors/4blocks

Cheryl Sigmon Four Blocks Column: www.teachers.net/
4blocks/column.html

K-12 Classroom Supplies: www.teachers.net/supplies
Unsubscribe Module: www.teachers.net/mailrings/
4blocks.html

The Teacher's Net Gazette: www.teachers.net/gazette
Related site: www.teachervision.com

ERIC

The Family Literacy Center at the ERIC Clearinghouse for Reading, English and Communication is posting its magazine *Parents and Children Together* at: www.indiana.edu/~eric_rec/fl/pcto/index.html

The New York Times Lesson Plan Link: www.nytimes.com/learning

SchoolNet: www.schoolnet.com

Classroom Theme-Study

BOOKS

Bromley, Karen, Linda Irwin-DeVitis, and Marcia Modlo. *Graphic Organizers: Visual Strategies for Active Learning.* New York: Scholastic, 1995.

Castaldo, Nancy Fusco. *The Little Hands Nature Book: Earth, Sky, Critters, and More.* Charlotte, V.T.: Williamson Publishing, 1996.

Chertok, Bobbi, Goody Hirshfeld, and Marilyn Rosh. *Learning About Ancient Civilizations Through Art.* New York: Scholastic, 1993.

Davies, Anne, Coleen Politano, and Caren Cameron. *Making Themes Work: Building Connections.* Winnepeg, Manitoba: Peguis Publishers, 1993.

Hansen, Jane, Thomas Newkirk, and Donald Graves, eds. *Breaking Ground: Teachers Relate Reading and Writing in the Elementary School.* Portsmouth, N.H.: Heinemann, 1985.

Hirschfeld, Robert, and Nancy White. *The Kid's Science Book: Creative Experiences for Hands-On Fun.* Charlotte, V.T.: Williamson Publishing, 1995.

Irvine, Joan. *How to Make Pop-Ups.* New York: Morrow Junior Books, 1987.

Jorgensen, Karen L. *History Workshop: Reconstructing the Past with Elementary Students.* Portsmouth, N.H.: Heinemann, 1993.

Meinbach, Anita Meyer, Anthony Fredericks, and Liz Rothlein. *The Complete Guide to Thematic Units:*

Creating the Integrated Curriculum. Norwood, Mass.: Christopher-Gordon Publishers, 2000.

O'Brien-Palmer, Michelle. *Great Graphic Organizers to Use with Any Book!* New York: Scholastic, 1997.

Perdue, Peggy K. *Science Is An Action Word!* Glenview, Ill: Scott Forsman and Company, 1991.

Strube, Penny. *Theme Studies: A Practical Guide.* New York: Scholastic, 1993.

VanCleave, Janice. *Play and Find Out About Science: Easy Experiments for Young Children.* New York: John Wiley and Son's, 1996.

Where to Find Theme-Related Materials

Many publishers offer a variety of theme-related materials. Contact the names below to receive their most current catalogs:

Demco, Inc.
4810 Forest Run Road
Madison, WI 53707
(800) 962-4463
www.demco.com

Dover Publications, Inc.
31 East 2nd Street
Minneola, NY 11501
www.doverpublications.com

Teacher Created Materials, Inc.
6421 Industry Way
Westminister, CA 92683
(800) 858-7339
www.teachercreated.com

T.S. Denison & Co., Inc.
9601 Newton Avenue South
Minneapolis, MN 55431
www.MHTeachers.com

Williamson Publishing
Box 185
Charlotte, VT 05445
(800) 234-8791
www.williamsonbooks.com

Parent-Community Connection

Cicciarelli, Joellyn Thrall, ed. *Parent Letters for the Primary Grades.* Cypress, Calif.: Creative Teaching Press, 1997.

Resources for Professional Development

Association for Supervision and Curriculum Development (ASCD)
1703 N. Beauregard Street
Alexandria, VA 22311-1714
www.ascd.org
Journal: *Education Leadership*

International Reading Association (IRA)
800 Barksdale Road, PO Box 8139
Newark, Delaware 19714-8139
www.reading.org

Journals: *The Reading Teacher; Reading Research Quarterly*

National Association for the Education of Young Children (NAEYC)
1509 16th St. NW
Washington, DC 20036
(800) 424-2460
www.naeyc.org
Journal: *Young Children*

National Association for Primary Education (NAPE)
University of Leicester
Queens Building
Barrack Rd.
Northampton NN26AF
Ph: 01604 36326
www.rmplc.co.uk/orgs/nape/index.html

National Center for Family Literacy (NCFL)
325 W. Main Street, Ste.200
Louisville, KY 40202
www.tpeyton@famlit.org

Newsletter: *Momentum*

National Council of Teachers of English (NCTE)
1111 W. Kenyon Road
Urbana, Illinois 61801-1096
www.ncte.org

Journals: *Language Arts; Primary Voices K-6; Voices from the Middle*

National Council of Teachers of Mathematics (NCTM)
1906 Association Dr.
Reston, VA 22091
www.nctm.org

Journal: *Arithmetic Teacher*

National Science Teachers Association (NSTA)
1840 Wilson Blvd.
Arlington, VA 22201
(703) 243-7100
www.nsta.org

Teacher Conference and Seminar Organizations

Staff Development for Educators (SDE)
10 Sharon Road
P.O. Box 577
Peterborough, NH 03458
(800) 462-1478
www.sde.com

Educational Publishers

AIMS Education Foundation
P.O. Box 7766
5629 E. Westover Street
Fresno, CA 93747

ASCD
1703 N. Beauregard Street
Alexandria, VA 22311-1714
www.ascd.org

Christopher-Gordon Publishers, Inc.
480 Washington Street
Norwood, MA 02062
(800) 934-8332

Creative Teaching Press
PO Box 2723
Huntington Beach, CA 92647
(800) 444-4287
www.creativeteaching.com

Crystal Springs Books
78 Jaffrey Road
P.O. Box 500
Peterborough, NH 03458-0500
(800) 321-0401
www.crystalsprings.com

Heinemann Educational Books
361 Hanover Street
Portsmouth, NH 03801-3912
(800) 793-2154
www.heinemann.com

IRA
800 Barksdale Road, PO Box 8139
Newark, Delaware 19714-8139
www.reading.org

NCTE
1111 W. Kenyon Road
Urbana, Illinois 61801-1096
www.ncte.org

Peguis Publishers Limited
318 McDermot Avenue
Winnepeg, Manitoba
Canada R3A 0A2

Richard C. Owen Publishers, Inc.
135 Katonah Avenue
Katonah, NY 10536

Scholastic
555 Broadway
New York, NY 10012-3999
www.scholastic.com/inschool

Stenhouse Publishers
477 Congress St.
Suite 4B
Portland, ME 04101
(888) 363-0566
www.stenhouse.com

Sundance
P.O. Box 1326
Littleton, MA 01460,
(800) 343-8204
www.sundancepub.com

Teaching Resource Center
P.O. Box 82777
San Diego, CA 92138-2777
(800) 833-3389
www.trcabc.com

The Wright Group
19201 120th Avenue NE
Bothell, WA 98011
(800) 648-2970
www.wrightgroup.com

Online Bookstores

Amazon: www.amazon.com
Barnes & Noble: www.bn.com
Crystal Springs Books: www.crystalsprings.com

Miscellaneous

Calkins, Lucy. *Living Between the Lines*. Portsmouth, N.H.: Heinemann, 1990.
Norris, Dennis. *Get a Grant: Yes You Can!* New York: Scholastic, 1998.

For information on having a "travel buddy" for your class:
www.rite.ed.qut.edu.au/oz-teachernet/projects/travel-buddies/index.html

The Responsive Classroom: www.responsiveclassroom.org